UTOPIA

UTOPIA

SECOND EDITION

Thomas More

TRANSLATED AND INTRODUCED BY
CLARENCE H. MILLER
WITH A NEW AFTERWORD BY
JERRY HARP

Yale UNIVERSITY PRESS / NEW HAVEN & LONDON

Published with assistance from the foundation established in memory of
Oliver Baty Cunningham of the Class of 1917, Yale College.

Afterword and Suggestions for Further Reading copyright © 2014 by
Yale University. Translation copyright © 2001 by Clarence H. Miller.

Yale University Press books may be purchased in quantity for
educational, business, or promotional use. For information, please e-mail
sales.press@yale.edu (U.S. office) or sales@yaleup.co.uk (U.K. office).

Designed by Rebecca Gibb. Set in Adobe Garamond type by Keystone
Typesetting, Inc.
Printed in the United States of America.

Library of Congress Control Number: 2012954304
ISBN 978-0-300-18610-9 (pbk.)

A catalogue record for this book is available from the
Library of Congress and from the British Library.

10 9 8 7 6 5 4 3 2

CONTENTS

INTRODUCTION

The circumstances under which More composed *Utopia,* as he recounts them in the opening of the book, give us some clues about one of its central issues: public service versus contemplative withdrawal. More was a busy London lawyer in the service of Henry VIII on a trade commission negotiating in the spring and early summer of 1515 in Bruges. In the midst of this activity came three months of leisure from late July to late October; the negotiations were interrupted because the Flemish ambassadors had to return to consult with their prince. Released from business and public service, More had time for thought and contemplation: he wrote what would become the second book of *Utopia,* a description of the island and its people, customs, and form of government—a sort of fantastic, Lucianic travelogue. After he returned home he wrote the first book, a semi-Platonic dialogue framework concerning the question of whether it is useful to serve as the counsellor of a prince.[1] The first book, in other words, argues about the alternatives of engagement or retreat.

Unlike Platonic dialogues, which reach solutions, or even Ciceronian dialogues, which are more open-ended but clearly suggest the superiority of one outlook, the first book of *Utopia* comes to no conclusion. It does not take long for the reader to see that Hythloday (whose name means "peddler of nonsense") contradicts his position by telling the story of his sojourn in the court of Cardinal Morton, who listens to Hythloday's advice about punishing thieves and suggests that it might be tried in a modified form. Nor does he defeat More in the argument about the necessity of communism; he simply evades it by insisting that More would agree with him if he had seen how communism has transformed the "good place," Utopia. But unfortunately the "good place" is also "no place." And not everything about the "good place" is good: apart from its policies on euthanasia and divorce, which might be tolerated in a non-Christian society, it practices capital punishment with a harshness not far from what Hythloday condemns in Book 1; its military and especially its colonial policies also leave much to be desired. At the end of Book 2 we are left with Hythloday's passionate condemnation of the outrageous social injustices of European society, but we are not really any closer to believing that they could be cured by communism, partly because we know that it has never been introduced in society as a whole and never could be, and we are never told how it was introduced or sustained in Utopia. Even if we thought it might work in Western nations, would we want to live in such a faceless and regimented society? The citizens sometimes seem like robots; the houses and even the cities seem almost interchangeable. Apart from Utopus, we never learn the name of a single Utopian. Did Hythloday never have any special friends there? One could say that he is not interested in autobiography but only in the Utopians' economic, social, and political institutions, but should children simply be taken from their parents and moved to a different family? Should whole populations be shifted back and forth to the continental colonies to provide demographic stability?

Such facts and questions make us realize that More's Utopia does not fit the ordinary meaning of the word as it came down in modern languages, where it signifies an unreservedly "good place" (though it still includes the notion that it is "no place," that it can never be actualized).[2] And More's *Utopia* should not be read (as it often has been and sometimes still is read) as presenting More's notion of a purely positive and desirable society. What the character More says was believed by the real More, though the character's range of opinion is circumscribed by the context in which he appears; the real More had opinions and ideas about issues the character does not address. The character argues at some length that it is reasonable and salutary to become the counsellor to a king—a problem the real More resolved for himself when he became a member of Henry's privy council two years after *Utopia* was first published. He also disagrees that communism would be a social panacea. He concludes by saying there are both good and bad features in Utopia: he says he disagrees with the Utopians' religious practices, their methods of warfare, and especially their communism, but, apart from communism, he does not tell us what specific features he disagrees with or why he does so. The real More does not have his character spell out these disagreements because the experience of the book is not supposed to give the reader a view of a perfect society or analyze what is good or bad about Utopia. Rather the work encourages taking a new view of social and political problems by seeing alleged (and strange) solutions to them and challenges readers to try to find out what they approve or disapprove of and why. To quote from Edward Surtz's acute and comprehensive introduction to an earlier Yale translation of *Utopia:*

> Is the success of *Utopia* due to dialogue? After all, dialogue is symbolic of open-mindedness, humility, and inquiry. Somehow or other, More succeeds in involving readers in the dialogue. It is no accident that *Utopia* ends with challenges. Is the Utopian view of war, religion, and communism really absurd? Is the Utopian vision really hopeless and unachievable? *Utopia* therefore is an open-ended work—or, better, a dialogue with an indeterminate close. More asks the right questions— which can never be answered fully.[3]

The central character of the book, and the real More's most original character, is of course Hythloday, who practically identifies himself with Utopia, to which he is unreservedly committed. His names suggest the bipolarity of his character. He is Raphael (God's healer), and Hythloday (the peddler of nonsense): on the one hand a passionate analyst of social injustice, an intense and outraged defender of the oppressed, the poor, the sick, and the weak, a proponent of freedom from crushing toil, an enthusiastic promoter of intellectual pursuits, a supporter of equal rights for women; on the other hand, he is an advocate of inhuman social engineering, colonial exploitation, assassination, bloody warfare (however brief), "ethnic cleansing" of the Zapoletes, and capital punishment for someone who commits adultery twice. He is narrow-minded, unrealistic, humorless, puritanical, stubborn, tactless, and—according to some of his critics—even self-indulgent and narcissistic. And yet he is an energetic, credible character, whom we do not find entirely admirable or entirely repellent, like Utopia itself. But also like Utopia, he is always intense and intriguing. He asks and answers important questions, and however much or little we may like his answers, he makes us aware of the urgency of the questions.

The way Hythloday speaks reflects his character and ideas, and some of the range and tensions of his style can be perceived even in a translation.[4] Hythloday's sentences range from turbulent and often strained complexity, when he is contrasting Europe with Utopia, to simple, straightforward ease when he is describing Utopia.

When Hythloday imagines a session of the French king's council and projects the advice he would give, he launches into a 464-word sentence—suspended, unrealistically intricate, almost interminable—and ends by asking More, "How do you imagine, my dear More, my listeners would react to this speech?" With wry understatement More replies in four words: "Certainly not very favorably." Well satisfied, Hythloday takes a deep breath and soars off into another imaginary council session about raising revenues, this time in a sentence of 926 words, a syntactical extravaganza so convoluted that he himself almost loses track of it. To Hythloday's concluding inquiry, More again replies with good-humored litotes and goes on to point out, in two- or three-line sentences, that the manner of advice is as important as the matter. Among editors and commentators, so far as I know, only J. H. Lupton has pointed out these strained, overburdened sentences, and until now among English translators only Ralph Robinson attempted to reproduce them. Nowhere else did More write

Latin sentences that so deliberately go beyond what ordinary Latin syntax can bear. And Hythloday does this precisely when he brings the ideal kingdoms of Achoria and Macaria, his anticipations of Utopia, into jarring and irreconcilable conflict with the military and economic corruption of Europe. The two worlds, ideal and real, collide and the ordinary syntax accepted by speakers of Latin cannot contain them.

Surely More expected his readers to be disconcerted, if not totally flummoxed, by these marathon sentences. It is not so much that Hythloday has lost his grip on reality; he understands French militarism and fiscal chicanery only too well, as the extensive commentary by Fr. Surtz will testify. Rather, his only reaction to real corruptions is to grip them in one hand and smash them into ideal solutions in the other. And the syntactic explosion leads us to the "ideality" of Utopia. As Richard Sylvester pointed out, "Hythlodaeus' argument . . . moves from a firm grasp on a past historical situation [the punishment of thieves discussed at Cardinal Morton's court], to a hypothetical revision of contemporary history [the French council set over against the Achorians], and, finally, to a totally aloof fabrication [the purely imaginary council on raising money and the Macarians, near neighbors of the Utopians]."[5]

When Hythloday describes his ideal commonwealth, his sentences undergo a remarkable change: they are predominantly brief, factual, straightforward, syntactically simple. Usually he is simply describing Utopian things as they are, and they are mostly simple, whether it be the doors of the houses,

There is no house which does not have a door opening on the street and a back door into the garden;[6]

or the selection of candidates for ruler,

For each of the four quarters of the city names one person and proposes him to the senate;

or the universal work at farming,

Farming is the one occupation in which all of them are skilled, men and women alike;

or the color of their cloaks,

throughout the island they are all of the same color, that of the natural wool;

or the shifting of people to maintain uniform populations,

This limit is easily maintained by transferring persons from households with too many people to those with too few;

or the distribution of goods,

And when it is distributed equitably to everyone, it follows that no one can be reduced to poverty or forced to beg;

or the lack of seeking for offices,

Anyone who campaigns for public office becomes disqualified for holding any office at all;

or their exclusion of lawyers,

they ban absolutely all lawyers as clever practitioners and sly interpreters of the law;

or their recruitment of soldiers,

In each city they choose troops from a list of volunteers;

or their strict keeping of a truce,

> When they make a truce with their enemies, they keep
> it so religiously that they do not violate it even under
> provocation;

or their withholding of honor and office from those who do
not believe in the immortality of the soul, divine providence,
and future rewards and punishment,

> they bestow no honors on such a person, they assign
> him to no office, they put him in charge of no public
> responsibility.

In such simple sentences, which I have rather randomly
sampled from the second book, everything seems so balanced
and rectilinear, so simple and straightforward, so effortless and
obviously desirable. And such simple sentences may tend to
lull us into simple unquestioning acceptance of what they say
as simple fact. They tell us what the Utopians do but leave
many unanswered questions about how they manage to do it.
How are the four candidates for ruler chosen in each quarter of
the city? What happens if someone is no good at farming or
refuses to do it? Or if someone dyes his cloak? Or objects to
being separated from his family and friends in a population
shift? How do you know whether someone is seeking an office?
The only sure sign is absolute refusal to accept it. In the absence of lawyers the judge is supposed to protect the interests
of the accused. But what if the judge dislikes the defendant
and admires the prosecutor? What if he is stupid? How was he
chosen? How was the prosecutor chosen? Are there no rules of
evidence? What if too few soldiers volunteer to fight? What
happens if, during a truce, the enemy ambushes a patrol?

What if someone has ambitions to be a magistrate but conceals them? What if he does not believe in the immortality of the soul but conceals his disbelief? How are the priests chosen? By whom?

Hythloday does not answer these questions. He considers them simply irrelevant because the difficulties they embody spring from pride, which has no place in Utopia. The institutions of the Utopians clearly cannot work unless pride is eliminated.[7] And how is pride eliminated? By the institutions, especially the abolition of private property. The institutions cannot be introduced unless they have already been introduced. But the ease and lucidity of Hythloday's sentences tend to mask such difficulties. The thing is simply there. No need to ask how it got there or can manage to stay there.

Naturally, Hythloday's syntax is not always so curt and pat, even in his description of Utopia, but when his sentences swell and become somewhat involuted and turbulent it is usually when he is contrasting the ideal life of Utopia with the corruptions of Europe, as when he condemns Europe's distribution of labor, or attitude toward gold or hunting, or futilely complex laws, or abuse of treaties, or the Zapoletan (that is, Swiss) mercenaries. But these are merely occasional aftershocks of the great quake of his marathon sentences in Book 1, and he soon reverts to the simplicity of Utopian syntax.

In Book 1 the length and complexity of Hythloday's sentences lead us to believe that More himself could agree with most of what he says until the approach to Utopia (by way of Achoria and Macaria) dissociates him from More, interrupts the debates about counsel and private property (leaving them unresolved), and frees Hythloday to present the simplicities of Utopia in simple sentences, which are so unlike More's way of thinking and writing elsewhere as to suggest that he meant us to probe them with questions—not only about obvious difficulties such as Utopian warfare, divorce, euthanasia, or colonialism, but throughout. So much of what the Utopians do is admirable, but how in heaven's name do they manage to do it?

There is, for example, a glaring omission in Utopia, which Hythloday's limpid and easy sentences may cause us to overlook: the political structure of Utopia has no central executive authority for its fifty-four independent city-states. Although the whole island has no single governor, it does have an annual senate composed of three wisemen from each city. If there were any real self-centered rivalry among these cities, even any normal conflict of interest, such a senate, without any executive machinery whatever, would be quite ineffectual. We, like More, have only to look to the city-states of ancient Greece or Renaissance Italy to see what would happen. Then, too, we are told about the punishments for various crimes in Utopia (among which the absence of theft may not be surprising, but what about assault or murder?), but, without a police force, who catches the criminal? Who checks whether he has the proper papers to be out of his own city-state? What prevents him from stowing away on a ship to the mainland? Questions proliferate endlessly. We are always being brought back to the basic paradox: the institutions cannot be introduced unless they have already been introduced.

Another remarkable feature of Hythloday's style, which is related to the deceptive simplicity of Utopia, is his diction. We are not surprised that he is fond of words like "equal" (which he uses 26 times) or "easy" (24 times). After all, his main thesis is that equality of goods makes just government easy in Utopia. But another group of frequent words suggests his inability to deal with specific problems in concrete circumstances and reflects the universalist, absolute, all-or-nothing cast of his mind: "all" (200 times), "nothing" (76), "none" (68), "whole" (62), "one" (35), "the same" (33), "any" (33), "no one" (29), "entirely" (24), "each" (19), "never" (19), "anything" (17), "everywhere" (14), "anywhere" (13), "only" (11), "universal" (9), "ever" (8), "never" (7). In the samples of short sentences given above, I made no attempt to include any of these words, and yet I noticed that they had inevitably appeared ("There is NO house"; "Farming is the ONE occupation in which ALL of them are skilled"; "Whoever seeks ANY office becomes ineligible for ALL offices"). Moreover, as I checked the instances, I found that they often tended to occur together with other words from this absolutist cluster.

A few examples must suffice to suggest the effect of such diction.

The island has fifty-four cities, ALL of them large and splendid and having EXACTLY THE SAME language, customs, institutions, and laws. They have the SAME layout and they look the SAME, insofar as the terrain allows.

From them [the storehouses] EACH head of household goes to get whatever he and his household need and takes away WHATEVER he wants, paying no money and giving ABSOLUTELY NOTHING in exchange for it. For why should he be denied ANYTHING, since there is plenty of EVERYTHING and NO ONE need fear that ANYONE would want to ask for more than he needs? For why should ANYONE be suspected of asking for too much if he is certain he will NEVER lack for ANYTHING?

On the other hand, here, where EVERYTHING belongs
to EVERYONE, NO ONE doubts that (as long as care is
taken that the public storehouses are full) NOTHING
WHATEVER will be lacking to ANYONE for his own use.
For the distribution of goods is not niggardly; NO ONE
is a pauper or a beggar there, and though NO ONE has
anything, ALL are rich.

Such reiterated universalist diction is the source of what
most readers feel to be objectionable about the Utopians: their
faceless anonymity and homogeneity. But such diction is not
characteristic of More himself, either as a character in *Utopia*
or in his other Latin writings. And it should cause us to ask
questions similar to those raised by Hythloday's simple sentences: how do you get everyone always to do the same one
thing everywhere, wholly and completely, without anyone
anywhere at all deviating significantly in anything, with no
exceptions, with no one ever wishing to contravene the universal system, with all in equal conformity, with never a dis-
senting voice, with nowhere a refusal to comply? Hythloday's
answer is one and the same, always: introduce Utopian institutions, based on the sharing of everything. Only then will everyone be totally and completely committed to the common
good (respublica). But only a people raised, educated, and
trained under Utopian institutions can make the institutions
work. As with Hythloday's simple sentences, we are brought
back to the paradox, the dilemma, the "double-bind": nowhere can such institutions be introduced except where they
have already been introduced—nowhere.

But Hythloday should not be viewed as merely narrow-
minded, solipsistic, and naive. When he condemns the injustices of Europe, his voice and his sentences are not incompati-

ble with those of More himself. His passionate denunciations of the greedy oppression of the poor and his compassionate indignation at the lazy, corrupt self-indulgence of the rich are intense and memorable; everyone remembers the sheep who were once gentle but now devour people (p. 22), or his thunderous peroration against economic and social injustice, culminating in the condemnation of the conspiracy of the rich who look out for themselves under the pretext of serving the commonwealth (pp. 132). Only when he flees such corruption and breaks through to the simplicities of Utopia do his sentences fracture Latin syntax and soar beyond what More's Latin, even at its most muscular, would attempt. And the simple sentences and universalist diction of his description of Utopia do not make him seem merely simple-minded. They also help him to make us think that this has happened, that it could happen (in spite of all our nagging doubts about how it could have happened or how it could happen in the world we know); and, even more, he makes us think that some of it should happen (in spite of the thought-provoking anomalies in Utopian behavior) because the Utopians really believe in the common good; and Hythloday makes us almost believe in their belief, and so we believe him even while we disbelieve him, just as (because of her virtuoso and contrasting styles) we believe and disbelieve his great compeer, the Folly of Desiderius Erasmus' *Moriae Encomium.*

THE EARLY EDITIONS AND THE LATIN TEXT
Erasmus and Peter Giles supervised the printing of the first edition (Louvain, 1516), adding commendatory and sometimes analytic letters from well-known humanists of the time; these letters, though they provide a useful context for reading

Utopia, have not been included in this translation because they are highly specialized and sometimes inflated. I have included More's prefatory letter to Giles and his second letter to Giles, which appeared only in the second edition, in 1517. Erasmus and Giles were also probably responsible for the marginal notes that appeared in the first edition, and they may have had a hand in changing some Latin proper and place names from Latin to Greek forms. In the early editions many of the marginal notes are merely labels to mark off sections equivalent to paragraphs (of which the early editions have none). I have omitted such paragraph markers and included only the marginal notes that make some independent comment on the text. I have supplied the paragraphing in this translation.

Thomas Lupset supervised the second edition (Paris, 1517), which was corrected by More. Erasmus transmitted copy for the third edition (Basel, March 1518), which was also corrected by More (sometimes differently from 1517). In fact, it is possible that More corrected 1517 later than 1518^m (as the March 1518 edition is known). The Basel edition of November 1518 was simply a reprint of 1518^m, as was the Florence edition of 1520. It is significant that More, Erasmus, and Johann Froben, the publisher of the Basel editions, originally intended to include the translations of Lucian by More and Erasmus, though they were never included because the volume had grown too large; Lucian's fantastic and satirical flair was one of the ingredients in the savory stew of *Utopia.* Moreover, 1518^m and 1518^n (the November 1518 edition) also included the Latin epigrams of More and Erasmus; several of More's concern issues of good and bad government.

The Latin text on which this translation is based is derived from all the texts and variants of the first three editions, the only ones in which More actually had a hand; these materials are presented in full in the comprehensive and definitive editions of Fr. Surtz and André Prévost. My Latin text corresponds very closely with the Cambridge edition of George Logan and others, which is the most accurate and usable modern text. For these editions see the list of books for further reading at the end of this volume. I have also consulted the remarks and emendations in the Latin editions by V. Michels and T. Ziegler (1895), J. H. Lupton (1895), and Marie Delcourt (1936).

A NOTE ON THE TRANSLATION

Since *Utopia* has been translated by Ralph Robinson, Gilbert Burnet, and several translators in the twentieth century, it may be asked why another translation should be undertaken. But the truth is that in spite of many translations, some of them frequently reprinted, *Utopia* has not fared as well as it deserves in English. Robinson's pioneering translation, published in 1551, is quite accurate (with only a few exceptions) and was usually consulted by subsequent translators, but it was made at a time when English did not yet have the strength, either in diction or style, to reproduce the elaborate Latin of *Utopia*. Hence his translation, though lively and vivid, often seems wordy and awkward (as it probably also did to his contemporaries who read Latin). But at least Robinson did not omit words or phrases when they were inconvenient, and he tried to match the varied style of the Latin. The same cannot be said for those who walked in his footsteps. By the time of Gilbert Burnet's translation in 1684, English prose was a varied and powerful instrument, fully capable of matching More's Latin;

but fashionable prose in the Restoration was simple, lucid, "easy" (in reaction against the florid, baroque "excesses" of the earlier part of the century). Hence Burnet streamlined and simplified More's Latin, ignoring its extreme stylistic variations, occasionally clipping and pruning it as well.

G. C. Richards, the first twentieth-century translator (1923),[8] tried like Robinson to be fully faithful to the Latin, in details and style, but he kept too close to the Latin so that his English often turned out to be awkward and unidiomatic.[9] H. V. S. Ogden (1949) explicitly mentions the translations of Robinson and Burnet, admitting that he has borrowed wording from both, especially Burnet. In fact his translation is swift and readable (like Burnet's) but only at the cost of simplification in detail and the suppression of elaborations in More's Latin. The same false tendency is carried even further in Paul Turner's translation (1965) and further yet in the translation by John Sheehan and John P. Donnelly (1989), who professedly simplify and prune the text for American college students. The translation by Robert M. Adams (1975) is also uniformly swift and breezy, and even its corrected form (1995) does not match the stylistic variations of the Latin.

In fact, More's Latin is often anything but colloquial and easy (pace Turner and Surtz). In his first letter to Giles, More describes Hythloday's language as unpolished, informal, and extemporaneous, giving his style the label "casual simplicity." But hardly anything in this letter can be taken at face value. When Hythloday speaks about Utopia itself his sentences are indeed generally simple and easy (Utopia is, after all, a simple and easy solution to social and economic problems), but when he denounces the corruptions of Europe in Book 1 and in the peroration to Book 2, his sentences are complex, lengthy, elaborate, muscular, even muscle-bound. Some translators seem to think that such complications are natural in Latin but not in English. But in fact, English can follow the normal complications of Latin well enough, and the unnatural complications in the Latin ought not to be merely smoothed out in the English. They are an important part of the meaning.

Hence I have tried to translate all the details of the Latin in idiomatic English that matches the simplicity, complexity, or even unnatural strain of the Latin.

1477
Born in London, February 7

c. 1482–90
School at St. Anthony's

c. 1490–92
Page in the household of John Morton, Archbishop of
Canterbury and chancellor of England

c. 1492–94
Student at Oxford University

1494–1501
Studied law in London

c. 1500–1504
To test his vocation to the priesthood resided in Carthusian
monastery next to his law school, Lincoln's Inn

1504–5
Married Joan Colt, late 1504 or early 1505

1509
Negotiated with Antwerp merchants on behalf of
London companies

1511
Joan, who bore him four children, died, and More
married Alice Middleton

1510–18
Undersheriff of London

1513–18
Wrote *The History of Richard III* in both Latin and English

1515
Member of a delegation sent to Bruges to revise
a commercial treaty

1516
Utopia published at Louvain

1517
Helped quell a riot by a mob of London apprentices, May 1

1517
Negotiated with the French at Calais and Boulogne about
suits arising from the recent war, September–December

1518
Became a member of the king's council and
Master of Requests

1520
Accompanied Henry VIII to a meeting with Francis I at the
Field of Cloth of Gold near Calais

1520–21
Negotiated with Emperor Charles V and the
Hansa merchants at Calais and Bruges

1521

Knighted

1523

In *Responsio ad Lutherum* defended Henry VIII against
Luther's attack

1523

Speaker of the House of Commons

1524

Moved into the large mansion he built upriver in Chelsea

1525

Chancellor of the Duchy of Lancaster

1524–25

High Steward of the Universities of Oxford (1524)
and Cambridge (1525)

1528

Commissioned by Bishop Tunstall of London to read and
refute Lutheran books in English

1529–33

Wrote seven polemical books in English against Lutheranism

1529

Attended the congress at Cambrai at which peace was
negotiated between France and the Empire

1529–32

Lord Chancellor of England

1534

Refused to swear to the Act of Succession because it
repudiated papal supremacy, April 13

1534

Imprisoned in the Tower, April 17

1534–35

Wrote *A Dialogue of Comfort Against Tribulation* in the Tower

1535

Convicted of treason on the perjured evidence of
Richard Rich, July 1

1535

Beheaded in the Tower, July 6

UTOPIA

On the Best Form of a Commonwealth
and
on the New Island of Utopia

a Truly Precious Book
No Less Profitable than Delightful
by
the Most Distinguished and Learned Gentleman
Thomas More
Citizen and Undersheriff[1]
of the Illustrious City of London

A Six-line Stanza on the Island of Utopia
by the Poet Laureate
Anemolius
The Son of Hythloday's Sister[2]

Called once "No-place" because I stood apart.
Now I compete with Plato's state, perhaps
Surpass it; what he only wrote about
I have alone in fact become: the best
In people, wealth, in laws by far the best.
"Good-place" by rights I should be called.

VTOPIENSIVM ALPHABETVM.

a b c d e f g h i k l m n o p q r ſ t u x y

TETRASTICHON VERNACVLA VTO/
PIENSIVM LINGVA.

Vtopos ha Boccas peula chama.

polta chamaan

Bargol he maglomi baccan

ſoma gymnoſophaon

Agrama gymnoſophon labarem

bacha bodamilomin

Voluala barchin heman la

lauoluola dramme pagloni.

HORVM VERSVVM AD VERBVM HAEC EST SENTENTIA.

Vtopus me dux ex non inſula fecit inſulam.
Vna ego terrarum omnium abſcp philoſophia.
Ciuitatem philoſophicam expreſſi mortalibus.
Libenter impartio mea,non grauatim accipio meliora.

b 3

THE UTOPIAN ALPHABET

A QUATRAIN IN THE UTOPIAN LANGUAGE

The literal meaning of these lines:
When I was not an island, the commander Utopus made me into an island. I alone of all the nations on earth, without philosophy, have presented to mortals a philosophical state. Freely I share what I have; not unwillingly I accept what is better.

Thomas More to Peter Giles, Greetings[3]

I am almost ashamed, my dear Peter Giles,[4] to have delayed for almost a year in sending you this little book about the Utopian[5] commonwealth, which I'm sure you expected within six weeks.[6] You knew, after all, that I was spared the labor of finding my matter, and did not have to give any thought to its arrangement; all I had to do was repeat what you and I heard Raphael[7] say. For that reason there was no need to strive for eloquence,[8] since his language could hardly be polished, first because it was informal and extemporaneous, and also because he is a person, as you know, not as well versed in Latin as in Greek; the closer my language came to his casual simplicity,[9] the more accurate it would be, and in this matter accuracy is all that I ought to, and in fact do, aim for.

I grant you, Peter, that with all this already taken care of, I was relieved of so much effort that there was almost nothing left for me to do. If this had not been so, thinking up the subject matter and arranging it might have required not a little time and study, even from someone of not inconsiderable intelligence and not totally without learning. But if I had been required to write not only accurately but also elegantly, no amount of time or study would have enabled me to do it. As it is, all these concerns, which would have cost me so much labor, are removed and all that remained to do was to write what I heard—not a difficult task.

But nevertheless, even to perform this trifling task, other chores left me almost no time at all. I am constantly pleading one case, hearing another, acting as arbitrator, handing down decisions as a judge, visiting one person or another on business or because it is my duty to do so; I am out practically all day dealing with others, and the rest of my time is devoted to my family, and so I leave nothing for myself, that is for writing.[10]

When I get home, I have to talk with my wife, chat with my children, confer with the servants. All this I count as part of my obligations, since it needs to be done (and it does if you do not wish to be a stranger in your own home); and you must do everything you can to make yourself as agreeable as possible to the persons you live with, whether they were provided by nature, chance, or your own choice, as long as you do not spoil them by your familiarity or turn servants into masters through over-indulgence. As I am doing such things, as I said, a day, a month, a year slips by.

When do I write then? And as yet I have said nothing about sleep and nothing at all about eating, and for many that takes up no less time than sleep itself, which consumes almost half our lives. The only time I get for myself is what I steal from sleep and eating. Because that is so little, I progressed slowly, but because it was at least something, I did make progress, and I sent *Utopia* to you, my dear Peter, so that you can read it and let me know if I have missed anything. For, though on that score I do not lack all confidence in myself (and I only wish that my intelligence and learning were a match for my not inconsiderable memory), still I am not confident enough to think that nothing has escaped me.

As you know, John Clement,[11] my young assistant, was there with us, for I do not allow him to miss out on any conversation which could be profitable to him because from this sprout which is beginning to grow green with proficiency in Latin and Greek I expect someday a marvelous harvest. He has made me feel very doubtful about one point: as far as I remember Hythloday told us that the bridge which spans the river Anyder at Amaurot[12] is five hundred yards long, but my boy John says that is two hundred yards too many and that the river is no more than three hundred wide. Please try to remember that point. For if you agree with him, I will go along with you both and believe I am mistaken. But if you do not recall, I will stand by what I think I remember myself, for just as I have taken great pains to prevent any inaccuracy in the book, so too, when I am in doubt, I would rather say something inaccurate than tell a lie, because I would rather be honest than clever.[13]

In fact, it would be easy to remedy this defect if you would find out from Raphael himself about it, in person or by letter. And you need to do the same concerning another difficulty which has arisen—who is more to blame for it, I or you or Raphael himself, I do not know. For it did not occur to us to ask, or him to mention, in what part of that new world Utopia is located. Indeed, to remedy this oversight I would be willing to give a sizeable sum, partly because I am ashamed not to know in which ocean the island lies about which I have recounted so much, partly because there are one or two people here, but especially one person, a devout man and a theologian by profession, who is amazingly eager to go to Utopia, not out of idle curiosity or any hankering after novelties but in order to nourish and spread our religion, which has made such a good beginning there. To do this properly he has decided to see to it beforehand that he is sent by the pope and made the bishop of the Utopians. He has no scruples whatever about begging for this bishopric, since he considers such ambition to be holy if it is not based on honor or gain but rather springs from piety.[14]

Therefore, my dear Peter, I beg you to contact Hythloday, either in person if that is convenient or by letter if you are separated, and see to it that this work of mine contains nothing false and lacks nothing true. And perhaps it would be best to show him the book. For there is no one else capable of correcting any errors and even he cannot do so unless he reads through what I have written. Then too, this will let you see whether he is pleased or annoyed at me for writing this work. For if he himself has decided to commit his labors to writing, he may not want me to do so. And I certainly would not want to deprive his narrative of the bloom and charm of novelty by making the commonwealth of Utopia public.

But in fact, to tell you the truth, I myself have not yet made up my mind whether or not to publish it at all. For the tastes of mortals are so various, the temperaments of some are so bitter, their minds so ungrateful, their judgments so preposterous that a person would do far better to follow his own bent and lead a merry life than to wear himself out trying to publish something useful or entertaining for an audience so finicky and ungrateful.[15] Most people know nothing about learning; many despise it. Dummies reject as too hard whatever is not dumb. The literati look down their noses at anything not swarming with obsolete words. Some like only ancient au-

6

thors; many like only their own writing. One person is so dour that he cannot abide jokes; another is so witless that he cannot stand anything witty. Some have so little nose for satire[16] that they dread it the way someone bitten by a rabid dog fears water. Others are so changeable that their approval depends on whether they are sitting down or standing up.

They sit around in taverns and over their cups they pontificate about the talents of writers, condemning each author just as they please, pulling him down through his writings as if they had grabbed him by the hair, while they themselves are safe and out of harm's way,[17] as the saying goes, because these good men have their whole heads smooth-shaven so that there is not a single hair to grab on to.[18]

Furthermore, some are so ungrateful that, even though a work has given them great pleasure, they still do not like the author any better because of it. They are not unlike ill-mannered guests who, after they have been lavishly entertained at a splendid banquet, finally go home stuffed without saying a word of thanks to the host who invited them.[19] Go on, now, and at your own expense provide a banquet for persons of such delicate palates and various tastes, who will remember and repay you with such gratitude!

Nevertheless, my dear Peter, raise with Hythloday the points I mentioned. Afterwards I will be free to consider the matter once more. But in fact, if he himself gives his consent—since it is late to be wise[20] now that I have finished all the work—in all other considerations about publishing I will follow the advice of my friends, and especially yours. Farewell, my dearest Peter Giles, with regards to your excellent wife, and be as fond of me as ever, since I am fonder of you than ever.

A Discourse
on the Best Form of a Commonwealth
Spoken by the Remarkable Raphael Hythloday

as Reported by
the Illustrious Thomas More
a Citizen and the Undersheriff
of the Famous British City of London

BOOK 1

Recently the invincible king of England,[21] Henry the eighth of that name, who is lavishly endowed with all skills necessary for an outstanding ruler, had some matters of no small moment[22] which had to be worked out with Charles, the most serene prince of Castile.[23] To discuss and resolve these differences he sent me to Flanders as his ambassador; I was the companion and colleague of the incomparable Cuthbert Tunstall, whom he recently appointed to be Master of the Rolls, to the enormous satisfaction of everyone.[24] I will say nothing in his praise, not because I am afraid that my friendship might seem to make me an unreliable witness, but because his virtue and learning are beyond my power to proclaim them and because they are everywhere so renowned and well known that there is no need for me to do so, unless I intend to display the sun by the light of a lantern, as they say.[25]

As had been agreed, we were met at Bruges by those to whom the prince had entrusted the negotiations, all of them outstanding men. Their leader and chief was the Mayor of Bruges,[26] a splendid man, but their spokesman and mastermind was George de Themsecke, the Provost of Cassel, who is not only a trained orator but also a naturally eloquent speaker; he is very skilled in the law as well, and also an extraordinarily deft negotiator because he is both intelligent and very experienced.[27] After one or two meetings we could not reach agreement on some points, and so they bade us farewell for some days and set out for Brussels to ask for the pronouncement of their prince.[28]

Meanwhile, as my business required, I made my way to Antwerp. While I was staying there, I was often visited by Peter Giles,[29] among others, though no other visitor was more delightful to me. A native of Antwerp, he holds a post of great responsibility and prestige (and he is worthy of the most prestigious), since for this young man it would be hard to say which is greater, his learning or his virtue.[30] For he is most virtuous and very widely read, and also good-natured toward everyone, but toward his friends he is so responsive, warmhearted, loyal, and unfeignedly affectionate that it would be hard to find even one or two anywhere that you would think comparable to him in every aspect of friendship. He has a modesty rarely to be found; no one is further from false poses; no one combines more prudence with simplicity.[31] Then, too, his elegant speech and his innocent wit are so attractive that his delightful companionship and his charming conversation alleviated my longing for my country, household, wife, and children, though I was tormented by my desire to see them again, for at that time I had been away from home for more than four months.[32]

One day, after I had heard mass at the church of St. Mary, which is remarkable for its beautiful architecture and its large congregation, when the service was over and I was getting ready to return to my lodgings, I happened to see Giles conversing with a stranger who was getting up in years. His face was sunburned, his beard untrimmed, his cloak hanging carelessly from his shoulder; from his face and bearing I thought he looked like a sea captain. But then, when Peter saw me, he came up and greeted me. When I tried to answer, he took me a little aside and said, "Do you see this man?" (At the same time he indicated the person I had seen him talking to.) "He is the one," he said, "I was just getting ready to bring straight to you."

"He would have been all the more welcome to me on your account."

"Actually on his own," he said, "if you knew him. For there is no mortal alive today who can give more information about unknown peoples and lands, and I know that you are very eager to hear about them."

"My guess was not far off, then," I said, "for when I first set eyes on him, I immediately thought he was a sea captain."

"But in fact," he said, "you were far off the mark. Certainly he has sailed, not like Palinurus, but rather like Ulysses, or even better like Plato.[33] This man, who is named Raphael—his family name is Hythloday—has no mean knowledge of the Latin language but is especially proficient in Greek; he has devoted himself to Greek more than to Latin because he has totally committed himself to philosophy and he knew that in that field there is nothing of any importance in Latin except some works of Seneca and Cicero.[34] Out of a desire to see the world he left to his brothers his heritage in his homeland (he is from Portugal),[35] joined Amerigo Vespucci, and was his constant companion in the first three of the four voyages which everyone is now reading about; but on the last voyage he did not come back with him. He sought and practically wrested from Amerigo permission to be one of the twenty-four who were left behind in a fort at the farthest point of the last voyage.[36] And so he was left behind in accordance with his outlook, since he was more concerned about his travels than his tomb. Indeed he often used to say, 'Whoever does not have an urn has the sky to cover him,'[37] and 'from everywhere it is the same distance to heaven.'[38] This attitude of his would have cost him dearly if God had not been merciful to him. However, after the departure of Vespucci, he traveled through many lands with five companions from the fort, and finally, by an extraordinary stroke of luck, he was transported to Ceylon and from there he reached Calicut,[39] where he opportunely found some Portuguese ships and at last, beyond all expectation, he got home again."

When Peter had told me this I thanked him for his kindness in taking so much trouble to introduce me to someone whose conversation he hoped I would enjoy, and then I turned to Raphael. After we had greeted each other and spoken the usual amenities that are exchanged when strangers meet for the first time, we went off to my house, where we conversed sitting in the garden on a bench covered with grassy turf.[40]

And so he told us how, after the departure of Vespucci, he and his companions who had remained in the fort gradually began to win the good graces of the people of that land by encountering and speaking well of them, and then they started to interact with them not only with no danger but even on friendly terms, and finally they gained the affection and favor of some ruler, whose name and country escape me. He told how, through the generosity of the ruler, he and five of his companions were liberally supplied with provisions and ships on the sea and wagons on the land—together with a trustworthy guide who took them to other rulers to whom he heartily recommended them. After many days' journey, he said, he discovered towns and cities and commonwealths that were very populous and not badly governed.

On both sides of the equator, it is true, extending almost as far as the space covered by the orbit of the sun there lie vast empty wastelands, scorched with perpetual heat.[41] The whole region is barren and ugly, rugged and uncultivated, inhabited by wild beasts and serpents and by people who are no less wild than the beasts and no less dangerous. But when you have traveled further, everything gradually becomes milder. The heavens are less fierce, the ground is green and pleasant, the creatures are more gentle, and finally one sees peoples, cities, towns, which not only trade continually among themselves and with near neighbors but also carry on commerce with distant nations by land and sea. From that point on they were able to visit many countries in all directions since there was no ship traveling anywhere in which he and his comrades were not eagerly welcomed.

He told us that in the first regions they traveled they saw flat-bottomed vessels, spreading sails made of wickerwork or of stitched papyrus, and in other places of leather. But afterwards they found ships with curved keels, canvas sails, and in fact all the features of our own vessels. The sailors were not unskilled in seamanship and celestial navigation, but he told us that they were extremely grateful to him for introducing them to the magnetic compass, with which they had been totally unfamiliar. For that reason they usually were afraid to commit themselves to the open sea and they did not venture to do so except during the summer. But now they have such confidence in the compass that they scorn the winter weather and are careless rather than secure; thus there is a danger that the device which they thought would do them so much good will do them great harm because of their imprudence.

To present what he told us about the things he saw in each and every place would take a long time and would be beyond the scope of this work. And perhaps I will speak of it else-where, especially those points of which it would be useful not to be ignorant, above all whatever correct and prudent provi-sions he observed among civilized nations. We asked him very eagerly about such matters, and he was quite willing to explain them, but we paid no attention to monsters, for nothing is less novel than they are. Indeed, there is almost no place where you will not find Scyllas and rapacious Celaenos and man-eating Laestrigonians and such prodigious monsters,[42] but it is not everywhere that you will find soundly and wisely trained citi-zens. But just as he noted many ill-considered practices among those newly discovered nations, so too he recounted not a few features that could serve as patterns to correct the errors of our own cities, nations, peoples, and kingdoms. These, as I said, will have to be presented elsewhere. At present I intend to relate only what he told us about the customs and institutions of the Utopians,[43] but first I will present the conversation which led him on, as it were, to mention that commonwealth. For after Raphael had very judiciously analyzed some of our errors and some of theirs (and certainly there are plenty in

both places) and had presented some wiser provisions both
here and there—and he had such a mastery of the customs and
institutions of every nation he visited that you would imagine
he had spent his whole life there—Peter was amazed by him
and said, "My dear Raphael, why do you not enter into the
service of some king, for I am convinced that there is none
who would not be extremely glad to have you, because this
learning of yours and your knowledge of peoples and places
would not only serve to delight him but would also make you
fit to inform him of precedents and aid him with advice. In
this manner you could at one and the same time promote your
own interests enormously and be of great assistance to your
relatives and friends."

"As for my relatives and friends, I am not much concerned
about them because I have done my duty by them well enough:
others do not give up their possessions until they are old and
sick, and even then they do so reluctantly, when they can no
longer retain them; but I divided my possessions up among my
relatives and friends when I was not only healthy and vigorous
but also young. I think they ought to be satisfied with my
generosity, and beyond that they should not demand and expect me to hand myself over into servitude to kings for their
sake."

"A fine thing to say," said Peter. "I want you to go into the
service of kings, not be in servitude to them."

"There is," he said, "only one syllable's difference between
them."

"But I am of the opinion," said Peter, "that, whatever name
you give it, it is still the course by which you can not only
profit others, both privately and publicly, but also make your
own position a happier one."

"Would I make it happier by following a course which is abhorrent to me? But as it is, I live as I please,[44] and I certainly suspect that is very seldom the case with the grandees of court. Surely there are plenty of people who strive to gain the favor of powerful men, so that you need not consider it any great loss if I and one or two like me are not among them."

Then I said, "It is clear, my dear Raphael, that you are not greedy for wealth or power; I respect and revere a person with your attitude no less than I do any of the high and mighty. But it seems obvious to me that you would be acting in a fashion worthy of yourself and of your noble and truly philosophical nature if you could bring yourself to apply your intelligence and industry to public affairs, even at the cost of some private inconvenience. You will never be able to do this to such good effect as you could if you became a counsellor to some great prince and urged upon him what is right and honorable, as I am sure you would. For the stream of good and evil, as if from a never-failing spring, flows from the prince down upon the whole people. And your learning is so complete, even if you had no great experience, and your experience is so full, even if you had no learning at all, that you would be an outstanding counsellor to any king whatever."

"You are wrong on two counts, my dear More," he said. "First about me, and then about the way things are. For I do not have the ability you attribute to me, and even if I had it in full measure, I would sacrifice my contemplative leisure to active endeavor without contributing anything to the common good. First of all, the princes themselves, almost all of them, are more devoted to military pursuits (in which I neither have nor desire any skill) than they are to the beneficent pursuits of peacetime; and they are far more interested in how to acquire new kingdoms by hook or crook than in how to govern well those they have already acquired. Moreover, among the counsellors to kings, there is none who is not so truly wise as not to need—or at least thinks he is so wise as not to tolerate—the advice of any other counsellor, except that they support and fawn on any and all absurdities propounded by the prince's favorites, whose favor they strive to win by flattery. Certainly nature seems to have arranged it so that everyone is delighted with his own insights. So the crow dotes on its chick, and the monkey on its whelp.[45]

"But in a conclave made up of those who envy the insights of others or exalt their own, if anyone should propose something which he has read was done in other eras or which he has seen done in other places, his listeners there immediately act as if their whole reputation for wisdom were at risk, as if they would thereafter be considered totally stupid if they cannot propose something to undermine the proposals of others. If all else fails, then this is their last resort: these things pleased our ancestors, they say, and would that we were as wise as they! And with this remark they take their seat thinking they have said the last word on the subject, as if it were a very dangerous matter if anyone were detected to be wiser than his ancestors on any point. In fact if those ancestors have instituted some truly excellent policy, we are quite content to dismiss it. But if they might have taken a wiser course on some point, we immediately and eagerly seize the pretext of tradition to maintain it. And I have encountered such arrogant, absurd, and captious judgments often enough in other places, but once even in England."

"What," I said, "you were in our country?"

"I was," he said, "and I spent some months there, not long

after the revolt of the Englishmen from the west against the king was put down with such a miserable slaughter of the rebels.[46] While there I was much obliged to the most Reverend Father John Morton, Cardinal Archbishop of Canterbury, and at that time also Lord Chancellor of England.[47] He was a man, my dear Peter (for More already knows what I am about to say) no more venerable for his authority than for his prudence and character. He was of medium height, not stooped over though he was of an advanced age. His looks inspired reverence, not fear. In company he was not standoffish, but grave and serious. Sometimes he enjoyed handling suitors roughly, but harmlessly, so as to gauge the intelligence and presence of mind each would display. He was delighted with such qualities, provided they were devoid of all impudence, since they were related to his own character, and he embraced them as valuable in getting things done. His speech was polished and pointed; he was very skilled in the law; his intelligence was incomparable; his memory was so excellent as to be prodigious. These extraordinary natural gifts he had improved by study and practice. The king seemed to rely very much on his advice and while I was there he seemed to be the mainstay of the commonwealth. This was not surprising: thrust immediately from school into the court at a very young age, active in important affairs throughout his life, continually whirled about by violent changes of fortune, he had learned practical wisdom in the midst of many and serious perils, and wisdom so won is not easily forgotten.

"One day when I happened to be dining at his table, a layman who was skilled in the laws of your country was there. Following up some remark or other, he launched on an elaborate encomium of the rigorous justice which was at that time

applied to thieves in England. They were executed everywhere, he said, sometimes as many as twenty at a time hanging
on one gallows,[48] and he remarked that he was all the more
amazed that the country was cursed to have so many of them
prowling about everywhere, since so few escaped punishment.
Then I said (and I dared to speak my mind freely in the
presence of the Cardinal): 'You should not be at all surprised.
For this punishment of thieves is both beyond the limits of
justice and not in the public interest. As a punishment for
theft it is too harsh, and even so it is not a sufficient deterrent:
simple theft is not so serious a crime as to deserve capital
punishment, and no penalty is great enough to keep people
from stealing if they have no other way to make a living. Thus,
in this matter, not only you but most of the world seem to
imitate bad teachers who are more eager to beat their pupils
than to instruct them. For heavy and horrible punishments are
imposed on thieves when it would be much better to make
some provision for their livelihood, so that no one should
labor under the cruel necessity first of stealing and then of
dying for it.'

" 'We have made sufficient provision for that,' he said.
'There are trades; there is farming. From them they can make
a living, as long as they do not willingly prefer to be criminals.'

" 'You will not get out of it that way,' I said. 'First of all, we
will overlook the many soldiers who come home crippled from
foreign or domestic wars, as they recently did from the battle
against the Cornishmen and not long before that from the
French wars.[49] They have sacrificed their limbs for the commonwealth or the king; their disability does not allow them to
practice their former trades and they are too old to learn a new
one. These,' I said, 'let us overlook, since wars happen only

now and then. Let us consider what is never not happening. Now there is a multitude of noblemen who not only live like drones on the labor of others[50]—namely the tenants of their estates whom they bleed white by raising their rents (for this is the only kind of frugality they recognize, and otherwise they are so prodigal as to reduce themselves to beggary)—but they also travel with a huge crowd of retainers, none of whom has ever learned how to make a living. As soon as their master dies or they get sick, they are immediately thrown out. For lords would rather support idle men than invalids, and often the heir of a dying master cannot support a household as large as his father's, at least at first. Meanwhile the outcasts vigorously starve unless they vigorously steal. For what are they to do? After tramping around a bit they will have ruined their clothes and their health. Disfigured as they are by disease and clad in rags, no nobleman will deign to take them in and no farmer dares to do so. For the farmers are not unaware that a person who has been brought up in idle ease and pleasure and who has been used to swaggering about like a bully, girt with sword and buckler, looking down his nose at the whole neighborhood and despising everyone but himself, is hardly likely to be a reliable and faithful servant for a poor farmer, working with hoe and mattock for miserable wages and scanty keep.'

"To this the lawyer replied, 'But this is precisely the sort of person we should cherish the most. For since they are more high-spirited and lofty-minded than artisans and farmers, they provide the strength and power of an army if we ever have to fight a war.'

" 'Indeed,' I said, 'you might as well say that we should cherish thieves for the sake of warfare, for you will never lack for thieves as long as you have the retainers. In fact robbers are no slouches as soldiers and soldiers are not the most lethargic of thieves—so finely matched are the two callings.[51] But this problem, though it is widespread among you, is not peculiar to you; it is shared by almost all nations. But France is infected with another pestilence besides, one that is even more virulent: the whole country is occupied and filled with mercenaries, even during peacetime (if it can be called that).[52] Their justification is the same as yours for maintaining idle retainers here: those foolosophers[53] think that the public welfare consists in having strong and stout armed forces in a state of readiness, especially veterans, for they have no confidence in untried troops, just as if they should seek out a war precisely to avoid having inexperienced soldiers, and people should be gratuitously slaughtered (as Sallust nicely puts it) lest hand and spirit should grow sluggish through inactivity.[54] Just how deadly it is to maintain such beasts France has learned to her cost,[55] and the same is made clear by the examples of the Romans, the Carthaginians, and the Syrians,[56] and of many other nations as well:[57] standing armies of mercenaries, on one occasion after another, destroyed not only their government but also their fields and even their cities. How little this was necessary is made clear by the fact that not even French soldiers, thoroughly trained in warfare to their very fingertips, can very often boast that they came off better than your draftees—not to put it more strongly lest I seem to be flattering present company.[58] But your troops, whether urban artisans or rough and untrained farmers, are not thought to be very much afraid of the idle retainers of noblemen, except for some whose physique does not lend itself to strength and boldness or whose brave spirit has been broken by the poverty of their families. There is little enough danger that those retainers whose vigorous and strong bodies (for noblemen do not deign to ruin any but choice physiques) are now either grown flabby with idleness or soft with almost ladylike activities, no danger, I say, that such retainers would be unmanned if they were taught a good craft to earn a living and were exercised in manly labors. However that may be, I certainly do not see that it can ever contribute to the common good to prepare for war (which you never have unless you wish to) by maintaining such a huge crowd of people who undermine the peace, to which we ought to pay so much more attention than to war. But this is not the only problem which makes it necessary to steal. There is another, more peculiar (so far as I know) to you Englishmen.'

" 'What is that?' said the Cardinal.

" 'Your sheep,' I said, 'which are ordinarily so meek and require so little to maintain them, now begin (so they say) to be so voracious and fierce that they devour even the people themselves; they destroy and despoil fields, houses, towns.[59] I mean that wherever in the realm finer and therefore more expensive wool is produced, noblemen, gentlemen, and even some abbots (holy men are they), not content with the annual rents and produce which their ancestors were accustomed to derive from their estates, not thinking it sufficient to live idly and comfortably, contributing nothing to the common good, unless they also undermine it, these drones leave nothing for cultivation; they enclose everything as pasture; they destroy homes, level towns, leaving only the church as a stable for the sheep; and as if too little ground among you were lost as game preserves or hunting forests, these good men turn all habitations and cultivated lands into a wilderness. And so that one glutton, a dire and insatiable plague to his native country, may join the fields together and enclose thousands of acres within one hedge, the farmers are thrown out: some are stripped of their possessions, circumvented by fraud or overcome by force; or worn out by injustices, they are forced to sell. One way or another, the poor wretches depart, men, women, husbands, wives, orphans, widows, parents with little children and a household which is numerous rather than rich, since agriculture requires many hands, they depart, I say, from hearth and home, all that was known and familiar to them, and they cannot find any place to go to. All their household furnishings, which could not be sold for much even if they could wait for a buyer, are sold for a song now that they must be removed. They soon spend that pittance in their wanderings, and then finally what else is left but to steal and to hang—justly, to be sure—or else to bum around and beg? For that matter, even as vagrants they are thrown into jail because they are wandering around idly, though no one will hire them, even when they offer their services most eagerly. For since no seed is sown, there is no farm labor, and that is all they are accustomed to. One herdsman or shepherd is sufficient to graze livestock on ground that would require many hands to cultivate and grow crops.

" 'And for this reason the price of grain has risen sharply in many places. Even the price of wool has gone up so high that poorer people who ordinarily make cloth out of it in this country cannot buy it, and for that reason many of them are out of a job and reduced to idleness. For after pastureland was expanded, huge herds of sheep were carried off by a murrain, as if God were punishing the owners' greed by visiting on the sheep a pestilence which might more justly have been hurled at the heads of their owners. But even if the number of sheep

23

should increase enormously, the price still does not go down, because, though the sellers cannot be said to have a monopoly since more than one is selling, still it is certainly an oligopoly. For the sheep have almost all come into the hands of a few, and these men are so rich that they are under no necessity to sell until they want to, and they do not want to until they get the price they want.

" 'For the same reason other kinds of livestock are similarly high-priced, and all the more so because, once the farmhouses have been torn down and agriculture neglected, there is no one to see to the breeding of animals. For even those rich landholders do not rear other animals as they do sheep. Rather they buy them lean and cheap in some distant market and then sell them dear after fattening them up in their pastures. And for that reason, I think, the full disadvantage of this system has not yet been felt. I mean that up to now they have raised the prices only in the places where the animals are sold. But when the time comes that they are taken from the breeders faster than they can be bred, then finally the numbers will also gradually decrease where they are bought, so that here also there must needs be a severe shortage. Thus the very feature that seemed to make your island extremely fortunate has been turned into an instrument of its destruction by the wicked greed of a few men. For these high food prices are the reason why everyone dismisses as many as he can from his household—to go where, I ask you, except to go begging or else, as a noble spirit can more easily be persuaded to do, to turn to robbery.

" 'What shall we say when this miserable poverty and want is coupled with wanton luxury?[60] For the retainers of noblemen, artisans, and one might say even some peasants and, in

24

sum, all classes of society indulge in extravagant sartorial display and excessive, luxurious cuisine. And then the cookshops, the brothels, the bawdy houses, and those other sorts of bawdy houses, the wine bars and alehouses, and then so many crooked games of chance, dice, cards, backgammon, tennis, bowling, quoits, don't all these quickly empty pockets and send their votaries off to rob someone? Get rid of these pernicious plagues, make laws requiring that villages and towns be rebuilt by those who have torn them down or be handed over to those who are willing to restore and rebuild them. Keep the rich from cornering the market and from having a licensed monopoly, as it were.[61] Let fewer people be supported in idleness, let agriculture be restored, let cloth working be reinstated as an honest trade which will give useful employment to this idle mob, whether those whom poverty has already turned into thieves or those who are now vagabonds or idle servants—in either case they will turn out to be thieves.

" 'Certainly unless you remedy these evils, it is pointless for you to boast of the justice administered in the punishment of thieves, a justice which is specious rather than either just or expedient. In fact when you bring people up with the worst sort of education and allow their morals to be corrupted little by little from their earliest years, and then punish them at last as grown men when they commit the crimes which from childhood they have given every prospect of committing, what else are you doing, I ask you, but making them into thieves and then punishing them for it?'

"As I was saying this, the lawyer was already getting ready to speak and had decided to employ that common method of disputants who are more diligent in repeating than in replying—so high is their opinion of memory. 'A very fine speech indeed,' he said, 'especially for a stranger who has only had more opportunity to hear about these matters than to get any precise knowledge of them, as I shall make clear in a few words. For first I shall recount in an orderly way what you have said; then I shall show on what points your ignorance of our affairs has misled you; finally, I shall rebut and refute all your arguments. Therefore, to begin with the first task I promised to undertake, you seem to have made four—'

" 'Be quiet,' said the Cardinal, 'for it seems hardly likely that you will reply in a few words after such a beginning.[62] Hence, for the present we will relieve you of the trouble of replying, but we reserve that whole task for you when you two meet again, which I wish to be tomorrow, if nothing prevents you or Raphael here from meeting then. But meanwhile, my dear Raphael, I would very much like to hear why you think theft should not be punished with execution, or what other punishment you would enact that would contribute more to the common good. For even you do not think we should put up with it. But if people rush into thievery now when it is punishable by death, and then if they could once be sure of their lives, what force, what fear could possibly restrain criminals? They would interpret the mitigation of the punishment almost as an incentive or reward for wrongdoing.'

" 'Most gracious Father,' I said, 'it seems to me to be entirely and absolutely unjust to take a person's life because he has taken some money. For a human life cannot be equated with the goods of fortune, not even the whole sum of them. But if they say that this punishment is redress not for money but for the transgression of justice or the violation of laws, would it not be right to call this extreme justice extreme injury?[63] For we ought not to approve of legal decrees so Manlian[64] that the slightest infraction causes the sword to be un-sheathed nor should we accept the Stoic maxim that all sins are equal,[65] making no distinction between killing a person or stealing a coin from him, for between these two crimes (if fairness means anything at all) there is no similarity or rela-tionship. God forbade us to kill anyone,[66] and are we so ready to kill someone because he has taken a bit of money? But if someone should interpret that command to mean that the power to kill anyone is taken away except when human law declares a person should be killed, what is to prevent human beings from using the same principle to decide to what degree rape, adultery, or perjury are permissible? In fact, God has deprived us of the right to kill not only others but also our-selves, but if the mutual consent of human beings to specific laws allowing them to kill one another has enough force to release their agents from the bonds of God's commandment and enable them, with no precedent from God, to execute anyone condemned to death by human law, will that not mean that God's commandment has only as much force as is granted to it by human law? And indeed on this principle human beings may decide to what degree God's commands are to be observed in all fields. Finally, the law of Moses, though it was harsh and severe because it was made for slaves, and stubborn ones at that, still punished theft with a fine, not death.[67] Let us not think that in his new law of mercy, by which he commands us as a father does his children, God has granted us greater license to be cruel to one another.[68]

" 'These are the reasons why I think this punishment is wrong. And I think there is no one who does not understand how absurd and even dangerous it is to society to punish theft and murder in the same way. For when a thief sees that he is in no less danger if he is convicted of theft than if he had also been condemned for murder, that consideration alone will drive him to kill someone whom otherwise he would only have robbed. For apart from the fact that there is no more danger if he is caught, murder makes him more safe and gives him a greater hope of concealing his crime, since the witness to it has been eliminated. Thus by using excessively harsh measures to terrify thieves we encourage them to kill the innocent.

" 'As for the usual question of what punishment would be more advantageous, in my judgment it would be quite a bit easier to find a better one than to find one that is worse. For why should we doubt the utility of that way of punishing criminals which we know was once preferred for so long by the Romans, who were quite expert in the art of governing? Those convicted of serious crimes were condemned to quarry stone or dig out ore, constantly shackled and guarded. But as for me, on this point I reserve my highest approval for the system practiced by a people generally called the Polylerites[69] whom I encountered in the course of my travels in Persia. Their population is not small and their institutions are not lacking in prudence; except that they pay an annual tribute to the king of Persia, they are otherwise free and allowed to make their own laws. But because they are a long way from the ocean and almost entirely surrounded by mountains, and because they are content with the produce of their land, which is by no means infertile, they neither visit others nor are visited very often themselves. In accord with the ancient policy of their country, they do not seek to extend their territory, and what they already have is easily protected by the mountains and the tribute paid to their overlord. They have absolutely no armed forces, their lifestyle is hardly splendid but it is comfortable, and they are happy rather than renowned or illustrious. Indeed, even their name, I think, is not very well known except to their immediate neighbors.

" 'And so, among them whoever is convicted of theft restores what was taken to its owner, not (as elsewhere) to the prince, for they consider he has no more right to stolen goods than the thief himself.[70] If the goods have been lost, their equivalent is paid from the possessions of the thief, and whatever is left is handed over intact to his wife and children. He himself is condemned to hard labor.

" 'Moreover, unless the theft was committed with violence, they are not shackled or imprisoned but left free and unconstrained as they work on public projects. Shirkers and slackers are not restrained with shackles but egged on with the lash. If they work energetically, they are subjected to no humiliation; they are locked up in their cells only at nighttime after roll call. Except for constant labor their lives are not uncomfortable. Since they are doing public works they are fed at public expense, and not badly, but in different ways in different places. In some places what is spent on them is collected as alms; and this method, though it is unpredictable, has nevertheless been found to be the most productive because the people there are compassionate. In other places public revenues are set aside for that purpose. There are places where they levy a tax on private individuals to support the prisoners. Actually, in other places they do not do public works, but when a private person needs workmen he goes to the city square and hires some of them for that day at a fixed wage, which is a little less than what a freeman would cost. Moreover, if a slave is lazy it is permissible to whip him. Thus no one ever lacks work. And over and above his keep, each of them brings something into the public treasury every day.

" 'They are all dressed in one color and they are the only ones who wear it. Their hair is not shaved off but it is clipped a bit short above the ears.[71] A little piece of one ear is cut off. Their friends are allowed to give any of them food, drink, and clothing of the right color. But it is death to give them money, both for the donor and the recipient, nor is it any less dangerous for a freeman to take money from them for any reason whatsoever or for a slave (for that is what they call the convicts) to lay a hand on a weapon. Each district has its own distinguishing badge, which it is a capital crime to throw away, just as it is to be seen outside the district boundaries or to say anything to a slave from another district. To plan an escape is no safer than to attempt it. In fact, to be an accessory to such a plan is death for a slave and enslavement for a freeman. On the other hand, rewards are allotted to informers: for a freeman money, for a slave freedom, and for either one pardon and amnesty for their complicity, to keep it from seeming safer to carry out a criminal plan than to repent of it.

" 'This law and the system I have described constitute their policy in this matter. It is perfectly obvious how humane and advantageous it is since vengeance is managed in such a way as to eliminate the vice and preserve the person, and to handle him in such a way that he has to be good and will spend the rest of his life making up for the harm he has done. Furthermore, there is so little fear that they will revert to their former ways that travelers who intend to make a journey consider no guides to be safer than these slaves, whom they exchange from district to district. For there is no opportunity whatever to commit robbery: they are unarmed; money is of no use except as evidence of a crime; punishment is in store for them if they are caught; and there is absolutely no hope of escaping anywhere. For how could a person whose clothes are totally different from anyone else's cover up his escape and disguise himself unless he ran away naked? And even then his ear would give him away. But couldn't they at least conspire to overthrow the republic?—that surely is the real danger. As if any district could hope to do so without sounding out and enlisting the slave gangs of many other districts! They are so far from being able to conspire that they cannot even meet or converse or greet one another. And then how can we believe anyone would dare to trust his companions with such a plot, since it is dangerous for them to remain silent and most advantageous to reveal it? On the other hand, if they are patient and obedient, if they give good reason to believe that they will lead reformed lives in the future, none need despair of regaining his freedom; indeed not a year goes by in which some slaves who have recommended themselves by their patience are not reinstated.'

"When I had said this, and had added that I saw no reason why this system could not be set up also in England, and with much more benefit than the justice which the lawyer had praised so highly, then he (namely the lawyer) said: 'This system could never be established in England without enormous danger to the commonwealth.' As he said this he shook his head, puckered his mouth, and fell silent. And everyone there jumped on his bandwagon.[72]

"Then the Cardinal said, 'It is not easy to predict whether the outcome would be favorable or not without at least trying it out. But when the death sentence has been pronounced, if the prince were to grant a reprieve without any right of asylum[73] in order to see how the system would work, and then if in fact it turned out to be useful, it would be right to establish it. If not, then thieves who had been condemned earlier could be executed at that time; on the part of the government this would be neither less nor more unjust than immediate execution, and during the trial period it would pose no danger. In fact, it seems clear to me that it would not be a bad idea to treat vagabonds also in the same way, for in spite of the many laws made against them, we have still made no progress.'

"When the Cardinal had said this, there was no one there who did not vie with the others in praising what they had scorned when I proposed it, but especially the part about the vagabonds because the Cardinal himself had added it on.

"I do not know whether or not it would be better to say nothing about what happened then, for it was quite silly. But I will tell it anyway, for it was not malicious and it has some bearing on our subject. A certain hanger-on was standing around.[74] It seems he wanted to play the fool, but he did it so well that he seemed to be one, raising a laugh with such witless jokes that the laughter was directed more often at him than at the jokes. But every now and then he came up with something not entirely absurd, so as to confirm the proverb 'Throw the dice often enough and you will sooner or later get a lucky combination.'[75] One of the guests said that in my discourse I had made good provision for thieves and the Cardinal had also taken care of the vagabonds, and now all that remained was to make public provision for those whom disease or old age had rendered destitute and who were incapable of returning to the jobs by which they had earned their living. 'Leave that to me,' said the hanger-on. 'I will see to it that this is also properly taken care of. In fact, I am desperately anxious to ship off this sort of person somewhere out of my sight; they annoy me so much with their wailing and whining and pleas for money, though they can never sing so pretty a tune as to extract a penny from me. Actually, one of two things happens: either I don't want to give them anything or I don't have anything to give. And so they have now begun to get wise. To keep from wasting their effort, they keep silent when they see me passing by. Good lord, they no more hope for anything from me than if I were a priest.[76] I would decree by law that all such beggars be divided up and parceled out among the Benedictine monasteries where they would become lay brothers (as they are called);[77] and the women I would order to become nuns.'

"The Cardinal smiled and took it as a joke, but the others took it seriously. A certain friar, however, a theologian, was so delighted by a joke aimed at priests and monks that he himself also began to make merry, though he was otherwise so serious as to be almost sour. 'But even this,' he said, 'will not free you from beggars unless you also look out for us friars.'

" 'But that is already taken care of,' said the hanger-on. 'For the Cardinal looked out for you marvelously well when he proposed that vagabonds should be confined and put to work, for you are the greatest vagabonds of all.'

"After they all had looked at the Cardinal and saw that he did not reject this joke either, they were not at all loath to enjoy it, all except the friar. Needled in this fashion,[78] he was indignant and furious (nor am I surprised that he was), so much so that he couldn't even refrain from hurling insults. He called the fellow a scoundrel, a backbiter, a sneak, and a son of perdition,[79] all the while citing terrible threats from Holy Scripture. Now the buffoon began to do some serious buffoonery, for he was clearly on his own ground.

" 'Do not grow angry, my good friar,' he said, 'for it is written, "In your patience you shall possess your souls." '[80]

"The friar replied (and I will give his very own words), 'I am not angry, you jailbird, or at least I do not sin. For the psalmist says, "Be angry and do not sin." '[81]

"Then the friar was gently advised by the Cardinal to control his emotions, but he said, 'No, my lord, my language springs from nothing but good zeal, as it should, for holy men have had good zeal, whence it is said, "Zeal for your house has consumed me,"[82] and we sing in church, "Those who mock Elisha as he goes up to the house of God feel the zeal of the bald man," just as perhaps this mocking and ribald rascal will feel it.'[83]

" 'Perhaps you are acting out of a laudable feeling,' said the Cardinal, 'but it seems to me that you would act, if not in a holier, then certainly in a wiser way, if you would not put yourself on the level of a fool and set out to cap his absurdities with your own.'

" 'No, my lord,' he said, 'I would not act more wisely. For Solomon, the wisest of men, says, "Reply to a fool in accord with his folly,"[84] as I am now doing, and I am showing him the pit into which he will fall[85] if he does not watch out. For if the multitude which mocked Elisha, who was just one bald man, felt the zeal of the bald man, how much more will be heaped on a single person who mocks a multitude of friars, for many of them are bald. And also we have a papal bull which excommunicates anyone who makes fun of us.'

"When the Cardinal saw there would be no end to it, he

sent the hanger-on away with a motion of his head and opportunely turned the conversation to another subject. A little later he arose from the table and, dismissing us, devoted himself to hearing the petitions of suitors.

"See, my dear More, how I have burdened you with a long discourse, and I would be quite ashamed of myself for doing so if you had not eagerly importuned me and seemed to listen as if you wanted no detail of this conversation omitted. Though I should have been more brief, still I did at least feel obliged to tell it to show how judiciously they scorned the plan when I proposed it and how the very same persons immediately reversed themselves and approved it when the Cardinal did not disapprove of it. Their flattery of him went so far that they seriously favored and almost accepted the ideas of his hanger-on because his master took them as a joke and hence did not scorn them. From this you can judge how high an estimation courtiers would have of me and my advice."

"Indeed, my dear Raphael," I said, "you have given me much pleasure, you told the whole story so judiciously and so deftly. Moreover, while you spoke I seemed not only to have returned to my homeland but also to have grown young again because of fond memories of the Cardinal, in whose household I was educated as a boy. When you honored his memory so highly, you cannot imagine how much dearer you became to me on that account, though you were already most dear. But I am by no means ready to change my mind yet. No, I am convinced if you could bring yourself not to shrink from the courts of princes, you could contribute a great deal to the common good through your advice. No duty of a good man (and you are one, of course) is more important than that. Then too, since your friend Plato thinks that commonwealths will be happy only when philosophers become kings or kings become philosophers,[86] how far will we be from happiness if philosophers will not even deign to impart their advice to kings."

"They are not so disagreeable as that; they would do so gladly. Indeed they have already done so by publishing many books, if those in power were prepared to accept their good advice. But undoubtedly Plato clearly foresaw that unless kings became philosophers, they would never give their approval to the advice of philosophers, because since childhood they have been thoroughly imbued and infected with misguided notions. He also found this out for himself when he was with Dionysius.[87] But don't you think that, if I proposed sound measures to some king and tried to eradicate from his mind the seeds of corruption, I would be banished or held up as a laughingstock!

"Come now,[88] imagine that I serve the French king[89] and sit in his council chamber, as the king himself presides in a secret session, surrounded by a most judicious circle of advisers who are very eagerly seeking out wiles and stratagems to keep Milan and win back Naples (which is always slipping from his fingers),[90] and then to overthrow Venice and make all of Italy subject to him,[91] and then to bring Flanders, Brabant, and finally all of Burgundy into his control,[92] and other peoples as well, whose realms he has long had it in mind to invade. At this meeting, while one urges that a treaty be struck with Venice, to last only as long as it suits the French, and that the French share their plans with them and even give them some share of the spoils, which they can reclaim when matters have been satisfactorily settled; while another advises them to hire German mercenaries, another to soothe the Swiss with payments of money;[93] someone else, on the other hand, thinks that his divine majesty the emperor ought to be propitiated with a votive offering, as it were, of gold;[94] while another thinks it best to strike a bargain with the king of Aragon, granting him the kingdom of Navarre (which belongs to someone else) as the price of peace;[95] and on the same occasion another suggests that the prince of Castile should be snared by the prospect of a marriage alliance[96] and that some nobles of his court should be brought over to the French side by giving them reliable pensions; when the greatest difficulty of all is encountered, namely what to do in the meantime about England; but they agree that a peace treaty should be negotiated with them,[97] for a weak bond should always be tightened by the strictest terms; let them be called friends but be suspected as enemies; and that therefore the Scots should be stationed in readiness, poised on all occasions to attack immediately if the English make any moves;[98] moreover, that some exiled noblemen be supported secretly (for treaties forbid that it be done openly) who can claim that the kingdom is rightfully his so that the French king will have a rein to check an English king he does not trust[99]—at this council, I say, amidst such a mass of suggestions, surrounded by such distinguished men, all vying to give advice about going to war, if such a nobody as I were to stand up and give an order to tack in a different direction,[100] expressing the opinion that Italy should be ignored and that the king should stay at home, that France is a kingdom so large that it is not easy for one man to rule it (much less should the king imagine he should consider adding others to it);[101] and then if I should put before them the measures adopted by the Achorians,[102] whose country faces the island of Utopia on the southeast side; if I should tell them that they had once fought a war to gain for their king a realm which he claimed to inherit because of some ancient marriage tie, and that, when they finally won it, they saw that they would endure no less suffering in keeping it than they did in gaining it, but rather that the seeds of war were always sprouting up, either rebellion within or incursions from without against the subjected people, so that they were always having to fight either for them or against them; that they never had an opportunity to disband their army, and that at the same time they were being stripped of their resources, their money was being carried out of the country, their blood was being spilled to provide someone else a smidgeon of glory, that they were no safer during peacetime; that at home the war had corrupted morals, imbued the citizens with a lust for robbery, that slaughter in warfare made them completely reckless, that they scorned the laws because the king was so distracted by trying to take care of two kingdoms that he couldn't concentrate on either one. When they saw that otherwise there would be no end to these great troubles, they finally took counsel together and very courteously gave their king the choice of retaining whichever of the kingdoms he wished; but they said he could not have power over both because they were too numerous to be governed by half a king (indeed no one is willing to share even a muledriver with someone else). And so the good prince left his new kingdom to one of his friends (who was soon afterwards banished) and was forced to be content with his old one. Furthermore, if I showed that all these abortive wars, which had thrown so many countries into turmoil for his sake would exhaust his treasury, destroy his people, and in the end still come to nothing through some mishap or other; and that therefore he should care for the kingdom of his ancestors, improve it as much as he could, make it as flourishing as possible;[103] he should love his own and be loved by them; he should live with them, govern them kindly and leave other kingdoms alone, since the kingdom which has fallen to his lot is enough, and more than enough, for him—how do you imagine, my dear More, my listeners would react to this speech?"

"Certainly not very favorably," I said.

"Let us proceed, then," he said.[104] "If counsellors were in a discussion with some king or other and were thinking up schemes to fill up his treasury, while one person suggests increasing the value of the currency when the king pays out money and decreasing it exorbitantly when he collects it so that he can discharge a large debt with a little money and collect a great deal when he is owed only a little;[105] while another urges him to pretend he is going to war and to use that pretext to raise money and then, when it suits him, to make peace with religious ceremonies, pulling the wool over the people's eyes and making them think that he is a conscientious, merciful prince who wishes to spare them bloodshed;[106] while another reminds him of certain antiquated, moth-eaten laws, long since fallen into disuse, laws which everyone ignores since no one even remembers that they were passed, and advises that he should therefore enforce them with fines, noting that no source of revenue could be more productive, none more honorable, since it has the appearance of a concern for justice;[107] while another advises him to prohibit many practices with heavy fines, especially those that are contrary to the public interest, noting that later he can make a monetary arrangement with those whose interests are hurt by the laws and that thus he can win the gratitude of the people and make a double profit, first from fining those whom greed has led into his trap and then by selling dispensations to others (the higher the price the better the prince, since he is reluctant to grant a private person the right to obstruct the common good, and therefore does it only for a high price); while someone else persuades him to put pressure on judges to rule in his favor in all cases and advises him to summon them to his palace where they are to discuss his affairs in his own presence, saying that thus no case will seem so flimsy that his judges (whether out of love of contradiction, or a desire to seem original, or a wish to curry favor) cannot, in his presence, find some loophole for a false verdict, noting that when the judges give differing opinions and argue about a case that is as clear as day, the truth can be called into question and the king will have a convenient handle to interpret the law in his own favor, pointing out that the others will acquiesce out of shame or fear and thus the judgment can be fearlessly rendered in court, nor can there be any lack of pretexts for someone ruling in the prince's favor, since he has on his side either equity or the letter of the law or a twisted interpretation of the language, or something that outweighs all laws in the minds of conscientious judges, the indisputable royal prerogative;[108] while everyone agrees completely with that saying of Crassus that no amount of gold is sufficient for a king, since he has to maintain an army,[109] and moreover that a king can do no wrong, no matter how much he wants to, since all the possessions of all his subjects, and even their own persons, belong to him, and since nothing belongs to anyone unless the king graciously refrains from taking it away from him, and that he should leave as little as possible to his subjects since his safety consists in keeping the people from enjoying too much wealth or freedom, which render them less willing to put up with harsh and unjust commands, whereas on the other hand poverty and privation break their spirits and make them patient, depriving the oppressed of the lofty aspirations needed for rebellion;[110] at this point, if I should stand up and contend that all this advice is both dishonorable and harmful to the king, for not only his honor but also his safety depends more on the people's wealth than on his own; if I were to show that the people choose a king for their own sake, not his, since his labor and effort enable them to live in comfort and safety; and that therefore a prince should be more concerned with the welfare of his people than with his own, just as it is the duty of a shepherd, insofar as he is a real one, to feed his sheep and not himself;[111] that experience itself shows how wrong they are in thinking that the poverty of the people is the safeguard of peace, for where can you find more quarrels than among beggars? who is more intent on changing things than someone who is most dissatisfied with his present state in life? or, finally, who is more driven to create a general disturbance in the hope of gaining something than someone who has nothing to lose? But if a king is so scorned and hated by his subjects that he cannot make them do their duty unless he harasses them with maltreatment, plundering, and confiscation and reduces them to poverty, it would certainly be better for him to abdicate his throne than to retain it by methods which may keep the name of authority but have certainly lost all of its majesty, for it does not befit the dignity of a king to rule over beggars but rather over wealthy and happy subjects; that was certainly what was meant by that upright and lofty spirit Fabricius, when he replied that he would rather rule over the rich than be rich himself.[112] Indeed, for one person to wallow in pleasure and luxury while he is surrounded on all sides by grieving and groaning, that is to be the guardian not of a kingdom but of a prison; finally, just as a physician is totally incompetent if he cannot cure a disease except by means of another disease, so too someone who does not know how to improve the lives of citizens except by depriving them of the comforts of life is admitting that he does not know how to rule over a free people; instead he should cure either his sloth or his pride, for these are usually the vices that make his people despise and hate him; he should live harmlessly on his own income, adapt his expenses to his income; he should curb crime and, by educating his people properly, prevent it rather than allow it to increase and then punish it; he should not be hasty to revive laws which are customarily ignored, especially those which are long disused because they were never desirable; he should never take something as a fine which a private person would not be allowed to accept because to do so would be criminal and deceitful. At this point, what if I told them that the Macarians,[113] who are also not very far from the Utopians, have a law requiring their king to swear formally and solemnly on the very first day of his reign that he will never have in his treasury at one time more than a thousand pounds in gold or the equivalent amount of silver?[114] They say that a king who was more concerned about the welfare of his land than about his own wealth made this law to prevent the heaping up of so much treasure as to impoverish his people; for he saw that this amount would be enough either for the king to fight against rebels or for the kingdom to repel a hostile invasion but would be too little to encourage him to invade other countries—and that was the primary reason for making the law. A secondary reason was that he thought it would make enough money available for the ordinary business transactions of the citizens; and since any money which accrues over that limit has to be paid back, he reckoned that a king would not seek out methods of extortion. A king such as this would be feared by malefactors and loved by his law-abiding subjects. If I should obtrude such notions and others like them on persons who are violently opposed to them, don't you suppose they would turn deaf ears as I told my tale?"[115]

"Deaf as a post, undoubtedly," I said. "And, by heaven I am not surprised, and, to tell you the truth, I don't think you should obtrude such speeches or give advice which you are certain they will never accept. For how can it do any good or how can such an odd discourse influence the thinking of those whose minds are prejudiced and dead set against such notions? In private conversation with good friends this academic philosophy is not unpleasant. But there is no room for it in the council chambers of kings, where great matters are handled with great authority."[116]

"That is what I said," he replied. "Among princes there is no room for philosophy."

"Yes indeed, there is," I said, "but not for this academic philosophy[117] which considers anything appropriate anywhere. But there is another sort of philosophy better suited to public affairs. It knows its role and adapts to it, keeping to its part in the play at hand with harmony and decorum. This is the sort you should use. Otherwise, during a performance of a comedy by Plautus, when the slaves are joking around together, if you should come out onto the stage dressed like a philosopher and recite the passage from *Octavia* where Seneca argues with Nero,[118] wouldn't it have been better for you to have a non-speaking part[119] than to jumble together tragedy and comedy by reciting something inappropriate? By hauling in something quite diverse, you would spoil and distort the play then being presented, even if what you add were better in itself. Whatever play is being presented, play your part as best you can and do not disturb the whole performance just because a more elegant play by someone else comes to mind.

"That's how it is in the commonwealth; that's how it is in the councils of princes. If you cannot thoroughly eradicate corrupt opinions or cure long-standing evils to your own satisfaction, that is still no reason to abandon the commonwealth, deserting the ship in a storm because you cannot control the winds. You should not din into people's ears odd and peculiar language which you know will have no effect on those who believe otherwise, but rather by indirection you should strive and struggle as hard as you can to handle everything deftly, and if you cannot turn something to good at least make it as little bad as you can. For everything will not be done well until all men are good, and I do not expect to see that for quite a few years yet."

"In that way," he said, "I would be doing no more than trying to remedy the madness of others by succumbing to their madness myself. For if I want to tell the truth, then I have to say such things. I do not know whether it is proper for a philosopher to say what is false,[120] but it certainly isn't for me. Though that discourse of mine might perhaps have been irksome and repugnant to them, I do not see why it should seem odd to the point of absurdity. If I were to describe everything Plato imagines in his *Republic* or what the Utopians do in theirs, these things might be better (as they surely are), but they might still seem strange, because here we have private property and there all things are held in common.

"As for my speech (except that those who have decided to run headlong down a different path cannot be pleased by

44

someone who calls them back and points out the dangers), but otherwise what was there in it that it is not fitting and even obligatory to say anywhere? Indeed if we are to avoid as odd or absurd everything that has been made to seem alien by the corrupt morals of mankind, we Christians will have to ignore almost all Christ's teachings, and he forbade us to ignore them, so much so that the teachings which he himself whispered in the ears of his disciples, he commanded them to preach openly from the rooftops.[121] And most of his teachings are far more alien to our common customs than that speech of mine was, except that preachers (following your advice, I imagine), whenever mankind refuses to make their behavior conform to the rule of Christ, adapt Christ's teaching to the behavior as if it were a ruler made of lead,[122] so as to make the two match in some way or other. I don't see what good that does except to allow people to be wicked with a better conscience.

"And that, indeed, is all the good I would do in the councils of princes. For my opinion would either be different, and that would amount to having no opinion at all, or it would be the same, and I would be the abettor, as Terence's Mitio says, of their madness.[123] For I do not see what you mean by that indirect approach of yours which you think enables you to manage things deftly even if you cannot make everything good, and at least make them as little bad as you can. For there is no room there to dissemble or to look the other way: you must approve of advice that is clearly quite bad and subscribe to measures that are utterly pestilential. Anyone who gave faint praise to wicked advice would be taken for a spy or perhaps a traitor. There will be no occasions on which you can do any good, since you have fallen among colleagues who will corrupt the best of men before they themselves will be reformed; either you will be depraved by their evil way of life or, if you remain honest and innocent, you will be made a screen for the wickedness and folly of others. That is how far you are from being able to improve anything by that indirect approach.

"That is why Plato, in a very elegant simile, explains why wise men are right to refrain from taking on governmental tasks: when they see people rushing out on the streets only to be soaked by never-ending rain and they cannot persuade them to get under a roof and out of the rain, they get under shelter themselves, knowing that they will accomplish nothing by going out except to get drenched together with the rest and considering it sufficient, when they cannot cure the folly of others, at least to remain in safety themselves.[124]

"But actually, my dear More (to tell you truly what I really think), it seems to me that wherever there is private property, where everything is measured in terms of money, it is hardly ever possible for the common good to be served with justice and prosperity, unless you think justice is served when all the best things go to the worst people or that happiness is possible when everything is shared among very few, who themselves are not entirely happy, while the rest are plunged into misery.

"Therefore, when I turn over in my mind the most prudent and holy institutions of the Utopians, who have very few laws[125] and yet manage so well that virtue is rewarded and yet, since everything is equalized, everyone has plenty of everything, and then when I contrast their customs with those of other nations, always issuing ordinances but none of them all ever achieving order, where whatever a person can get he calls his own private property, where a mass of laws, enacted day after day, are never enough to ensure that anyone can protect what each calls his own private property or even adequately distinguish it from what belongs to someone else (as can easily be seen from the infinite lawsuits which are always being filed and are never finished), when I consider these things, I say, I have a higher opinion of Plato and I am not surprised that he would not deign to make any laws for people who would not accept laws requiring that all goods be shared equally by all. In his great wisdom he easily foresaw that the one and only path to the welfare of the public is the equal allocation of goods; and I doubt whether such equality can be maintained where every individual has his own property.[126] For where everyone tries to get clear title to whatever he can scrape together, then however abundant things are, a few men divide up everything among themselves, leaving everyone else in poverty. And it usually happens that each sort deserves the lot of the other, since the one is rapacious, wicked, and worthless, and the other is made up of simple, modest men who by their daily labor contribute more to the common good than to themselves.

"Thus I am firmly persuaded that there is no way property can be equitably and justly distributed or the affairs of mortal men managed so as to make them happy unless private property is utterly abolished. But if it remains, there will also always remain a distressing and unavoidable burden of poverty and anxiety on the backs of the largest and best part of the human race. I grant their misery may be somewhat alleviated but I contend that it cannot be fully eliminated. I mean, if you decreed that no one could own more than a certain amount of land and that there be a legal limit to the money anyone can possess, if some laws were enacted that could keep the prince from being too powerful or the people too headstrong, that would keep offices from being solicited or put up for sale, or keep them from entailing many expenses (for otherwise they

47

provide opportunities to rake in money by fraud and spolia-
tion or it becomes necessary to put rich men in offices which
ought to be held by wise men), such laws, I say, could mitigate
and alleviate these ills, just as applying continual poultices can
relieve the symptoms of sick bodies that are beyond healing.
But as long as everyone has his own property, there is no hope
whatever of curing them and putting society back into good
condition. In fact, while you are trying to cure one part you ag-
gravate the malady in other parts; curing one disease causes another to break out in its place, since you cannot give something
to one person without taking it away from someone else."

"Quite the contrary," I said, "it seems to me that no one can
live comfortably where everything is held in common. For how
can there be any abundance of goods when everyone stops
working because he is no longer motivated by making a profit,
and grows lazy because he relies on the labors of others. And
then, when people are driven by want and there is no law which
enables them to keep their acquisitions for their own use,
wouldn't everyone necessarily suffer from continual bloodshed
and turmoil? Especially when the magistrates no longer have
any respect or authority, for I cannot conceive how they could
have any among people who are all placed on one level."[127]

"I am not surprised that you think so," he said, "since you
have no conception of the matter, or only a false one. But if
you had been with me in Utopia and had seen their customs
and institutions in person as I did (for I lived there more than
five years, and I would never have wanted to leave except
to reveal that new world to others) you would quite agree
that you had never seen a people well governed anywhere but
there."

"But you would surely have a hard time persuading me,"

said Peter Giles, "that a better governed people can be found in that new world than in the one we know, since our intellects are no worse than theirs and our governments are older, I imagine, than theirs, so that long experience has brought to light many features which make our lives more comfortable, to say nothing of some things we have discovered by chance which no amount of ingenuity would have sufficed to invent."

"As for the antiquity of governments," said Raphael, "you could give a more accurate judgment if you had read through the histories of that world: if they are trustworthy, there were cities there before there were people here. As for what ingenuity has invented or chance revealed up till now, that could have happened in either place. But certainly I think that even though we may surpass them in intelligence, they still leave us far behind in diligence and zeal to learn.

"According to their chronicles before we landed there they had never heard anything about us Ultra-equatorials (for that is what they call us) except that some twelve hundred years ago a ship was driven to Utopia by a storm and shipwrecked there. Some Romans and Egyptians were cast upon the shore and never left there again. Notice how their diligence turned this single occasion to their advantage. There was no useful skill in the whole Roman empire which they did not learn from the explanations of the strangers or did not manage to discover from the hints and clues they were given. Such was the enormous gain they made on this one occasion when some men from here were driven to their shores. But if a similar accident ever brought one of them from there to here, the incident has been completely forgotten, just as posterity perhaps will also forget that I was once there. One meeting alone was enough for them to appropriate all of our useful inventions, but I think it will be a long time before we will accept any institution of theirs which is better than ours. And I think that is the only reason why they manage their affairs more prudently and live more happily than we do, though we are not inferior to them in intelligence or resources."

"Therefore, my dear Raphael," I said, "I beg and implore you, describe the island to us. And do not try to be brief but explain in order their fields, rivers, cities, population, customs, institutions, laws, and, in short, whatever you think we would want to know. And you should think we want to know whatever we don't know yet."

"There is nothing I would rather do," he said, "for I have all this at my fingertips. But it will take some free time."

"Then let us go inside to eat lunch," I said. "Afterwards we will take as much time as we want."

"Agreed," he said. And so we went in to eat lunch. After lunch we came back to the same place and sat down on the same bench, and having instructed the servants that we were not to be interrupted, Peter Giles and I urged Raphael to keep his promise. When he saw that we were attentive and eager to hear, he sat there quiet and thoughtful for a little while, and then began as follows.

THE END OF THE FIRST BOOK

The Discourse of Raphael Hythloday
on the Best Form of a Commonwealth

as Reported by
Thomas More, Undersheriff of London

BOOK 2

The island of the Utopians is two hundred miles across in the middle, where it is widest, and throughout most of the island it is not much narrower, but toward both ends it narrows a bit. These ends, curling around into a circle with a circumference of five hundred miles, make the whole island look like a new moon. The sea flows in between the horns through a strait about eleven miles wide and then spreads out into a huge empty space protected from the wind on all sides, like an enormous, smooth, unruffled lake; thus almost the whole inner coast serves as a harbor and allows ships to go from shore to shore in all directions, much to the advantage of the people. The jaws of the strait are dangerous, on one side because of shallows, on the other because of rocks. In just about the middle of the channel, one rock stands out, visible and hence harmless; they have built and garrisoned a tower on it. The other rocks are hidden and treacherous. The channels are known only to the Utopians themselves, and hence it hardly ever happens that a foreigner enters the bay without a Utopian

Amauroti vrbs.

fons Anydri.

Ostium anydri.

Hythlodaeus.

MAP OF UTOPIA,
WOODCUT FROM THE NOVEMBER 1518 EDITION
(Beinecke Rare Book and Manuscript Library, Yale University)

pilot. Indeed they themselves find it hard to enter it safely, except that they set their course by means of some signals on the shore. By moving these to different locations, they can easily lure an enemy fleet to shipwreck, no matter how large it is.

On the outside coast there are not a few ports. But everywhere the landing places are so well defended, either naturally or artificially, that a few troops can keep a huge army from coming ashore. According to report, however (and the appearance of the place bears it out), their land was once not surrounded by the ocean. But Utopus, who conquered the island and named it after himself (for before that time it had been called Abraxa)[128] and who brought its crude and rustic mob to a level of culture and humanity beyond almost all other mortals, after he won the victory at his first assault, had a channel cut fifteen miles wide at the point where the land adjoined the continent, and thus caused the sea to flow all around the land.[129] And since he set not only the inhabitants to this task but also employed his own soldiers (to keep the inhabitants from thinking the work was imposed on them as a humiliation), the labor was shared by a great multitude of workers and was finished in an incredibly short time,[130] so that the neighboring peoples (who at first ridiculed the project as silly) were overwhelmed with wonder and fear.

The island has fifty-four cities,[131] all of them large and splendid and having exactly the same language, customs, institutions, and laws. They have the same layout and they look the same, insofar as the terrain allows.[132] Those which are closest to each other are separated by twenty-four miles. None is so isolated that it is more than a day's journey on foot from another city. Every year each city sends three old and experienced citizens to Amaurot to discuss problems common to the whole island. For that city, which is located at the navel of the land, so to speak, and hence is most convenient as a meeting place for the delegates from everywhere, is the capital and chief city.

The land is so well distributed that no city has less than twelve miles of ground on all sides, though it may have much more in some directions, namely where the cities are furthest apart from one another. None of them is driven by any desire to extend its boundaries.[133] Indeed, whatever land they have, they consider themselves its tenant-farmers, not its landlords. In the countryside, throughout the fields, they have conveniently located houses, each provided with farming tools. They are inhabited by the citizens, who take turns going out to live there. No country household has fewer than forty men and women, besides the two slaves bound to the land; it is presided over by a master and mistress who are sober and mature. Every thirty households are ruled by one phylarch.[134] Every year twenty from each household return to the city, having fulfilled their two-year stint in the country. They are replaced by twenty substitutes from the city, who are to be trained by those who have already been there a year and hence are more skilled in farmwork; the substitutes themselves will train another group the following year, for if everyone were new and equally ignorant of farming, the crops would suffer from lack of skill. Although this system of exchanging farmers is customary, to keep anyone from being forced to live this hard life for a long time, nevertheless many who have a natural bent for agricultural pursuits apply for and are allowed additional years.

They farm the land, raise cattle, cut wood, and convey it to the cities by the most convenient route, whether by sea or by land. They raise a huge number of chickens, and they have a marvelous method of doing it. The hens do not sit on the eggs. For the Utopians themselves tend a great number of eggs, keeping them alive and hatching them in constant warmth.[135] As soon as the chicks emerge from the shell, they recognize and follow human beings around as if they were their mothers.

They raise very few horses and none but high-spirited ones, which serve no other purpose than the training of young people in horsemanship. For ploughing and hauling they use oxen; they grant that they are inferior to horses in short sprints, but they consider them superior over the long haul and less subject to diseases; moreover, they require less effort and expense to maintain, and when they have served out their term, they can be used for food.

Grain they use only for bread.[136] For they drink either wine made from grapes or cider made from apples or pears or else plain water, which they often boil with honey or licorice, of which they have plenty. Although they know (and they know it very well) how much produce is needed by a city and its surrounding population, they plant far more grain and raise far more cattle than they need for their own use, giving the surplus to their neighbors. All the supplies that are necessary but not available in the country they get from the city, giving nothing in exchange; the city magistrates provide them the goods with no bargaining. For every month many of them gather there on the feast day. On the day of harvesting, the phylarchs of the farmers inform the city magistrates how many citizens should be sent out; since they arrive at precisely the right time, such a large crowd of workers gets the harvest almost completely done in one day if they have good weather.[137]

THEIR CITIES, ESPECIALLY AMAUROT

If you know one of their cities, you know them all, so similar are they in all respects (so far as the terrain allows). And so I will describe one of them (it doesn't much matter which one). But why choose any one except Amaurot? For it is the most notable and takes precedence over the others because the senate meets there; and no other is better known to me, since I lived there for five whole years.

Amaurot, then, is situated on the gentle slope of a mountain; its shape is almost square. Beginning almost at the crest of the hill, it stretches two miles down to the river Anyder;[138] its width is slightly greater along the river than it is at the hilltop. The source of the Anyder is eighty miles above Amaurot, a small spring which is amplified by tributaries, two of them sizeable, until, when it reaches the city itself, it is five hundred yards wide. Then for sixty miles it flows on, getting wider and finally flowing into the ocean. In the space between the city and the coast, and also for some miles above the city, the tide flows and ebbs for six whole hours in a swift current. Seawater flows in to a point thirty miles upstream, filling the whole channel of the Anyder and driving the river water upstream.[139] It also makes the water salty somewhat higher up; from there the river gradually grows fresh and it is pure when it flows by the city. And at ebb tide it flows pure and fresh nearly all the way to the mouth of the river.

The city is connected to the opposite bank of the river by a bridge made not of pilings and planks but of beautifully arched stonework; it is placed at a point furthest from the sea so that ships can sail unobstructed along that whole side of the city.[140] They also have another stream, not large but very gentle and pleasant, which gushes from a spring on the same mountain where the city is located; it flows down through the middle of the city into the Anyder. The Amaurotians have fortified the head and spring of this stream, which is located a little outside the city, surrounding it with walls that link it to the city, so that if an enemy ever attacks them, the water cannot be diverted or contaminated. From this stream the water is channeled in tile conduits to the various districts in the lower parts of the city. Where the terrain makes this impossible, rainwater collected in large cisterns serves the same purpose.

The city is surrounded by a high, thick wall with many towers and bastions. On three sides the wall is surrounded by a moat that is dry but wide and deep and blocked by thorn hedges; on the fourth side the river itself serves as a moat. The streets are laid out to facilitate traffic and to offer protection from the wind. The buildings are by no means ugly; the houses extend in a continuous row along the whole block, facing the row on the other side of the street; the housefronts along each block are separated by a street twenty feet wide. Behind the houses, a large garden, as long on each side as the block itself, is hemmed in on all sides by the backs of the rowhouses.

There is no house which does not have a door opening on the street and a backdoor into the garden. The double doors, which open easily with a push of the hand and close again automatically, allow anyone to come in—so there is nothing private anywhere.[141] For every ten years they exchange the houses themselves by drawing lots. The Utopians place great stock by these gardens; in them they grow vines, fruit trees, herbs, and flowers, all so bright and well tended that I have never seen anything more flourishing and elegant. In gardening they are motivated not only by their own pleasure but also by competition among the various blocks to see which has the best garden. And certainly you will not easily find any feature of the whole city that is of greater use to the citizens or gives them more pleasure.[142] For that reason the founder of the city seems to have devoted more attention to these gardens than he did to anything else.

For they say that in the very beginning Utopus himself laid out the whole plan of the city. But he left it to succeeding ages to complete the adornment and landscaping that could not be completed during one lifetime. Thus in their annals, which have been diligently and scrupulously kept up since the island was captured 1,760 years ago,[143] it is recorded that at first their dwellings were humble, mere huts and shacks, built of wood gathered at random, the walls plastered with mud. The roofs came to a point and were thatched with straw. But now all houses have a handsome appearance and are built three stories high. The outer sections of the walls are made of fieldstone, quarried rock, or brick, and the space between is filled up with gravel and cement. The roofs are flat and are coated with a sort of plaster which is not expensive but is formulated so as to be fireproof and more weather-resistant than lead.[144] They commonly use glass (which is very plentiful there) to keep out the wind; sometimes they also use thin linen, soaked in clear oil or treated with resin—a method which has two advantages: it lets in more light and keeps out more drafts.[145]

THEIR MAGISTRATES

Every year each group of thirty families elects its magistrate, who in their ancient language was called a syphogrant but is known as a phylarch in the modern tongue. Ten syphogrants with their households are presided over by an official once called a tranibor, now known as a protophylarch.[146] Finally, all the syphogrants, who number two hundred,[147] having sworn to choose the person they consider the most capable, elect the ruler by secret ballot, choosing him from the four candidates named by the people.[148] For each of the four quarters of the city names one person and proposes him to the senate. The ruler remains in office for life, unless his tenure is interrupted because he is suspected of trying to become a tyrant.[149] They elect the tranibors every year, but they do not lightly change them. All the other magistrates hold office for one year.[150]

Every third day, and sometimes oftener if circumstances require it, the tranibors gather to advise the ruler. They make decisions about public affairs; if there are any disputes among private persons (and there are very few) they settle them in a timely fashion.[151] They always invite two syphogrants into the senate, different ones on every occasion; and they have provided that no measures concerning public affairs be adopted unless they have been discussed in the senate three days before a decision is reached.[152] To enter into schemes concerning affairs of state outside the senate or public assemblies is a capital crime. These measures were taken, they say, to make it hard for the ruler and the tranibors to conspire to change the form of government and set up a tyranny over the people. And for the same reason matters of great moment are presented at the assemblies of the syphogrants, who report the matter to the households, take counsel among themselves, and report their recommendations to the senate. Sometimes a matter will be referred to the council of the whole island.[153]

Then, too, the senate has a rule that no point is discussed on the same day it is brought up, but rather it is put off till the next meeting;[154] they do this so that someone who blurts out the first thing that occurs to him will not proceed to think up arguments to defend his position instead of looking for what is of use to the commonwealth, being willing to damage the public welfare rather than his own reputation, ashamed, as it were, in a perverse and wrong-headed way, to admit that his first view was short-sighted.[155] From the start such a person should have taken care to speak with deliberation rather than haste.

OCCUPATIONS

Farming is the one occupation in which all of them are skilled, men and women alike.[156] They are all trained in it from childhood on, partly by instruction in the classroom, partly by being taken out to play at it,[157] as it were, in the fields near the city, not merely looking on but doing the work themselves for bodily exercise.

Besides farming (which, as I said, is common to all of them) everyone is taught some trade of his own. The ordinary ones are working with wool or linen or laboring as a stone mason, blacksmith, or carpenter. No other trade there employs any number worth mentioning.[158] As for their clothing—which is uniform throughout the island for all age groups and varies only to indicate sex or marital status, and which is not unappealing to the eye, allows freedom of movement, and is adapted to either heat or cold—as for their clothing, I say, each household makes its own.

Everybody learns one or the other of these trades, including women as well as men. But women, as the weaker sex, engage in lighter crafts, mostly working with wool or linen. The other trades, which require more strength, are relegated to the men. Generally children take up their father's trade, for most are naturally inclined to it.[159] But if anyone is drawn to another occupation, he is transferred by adoption into another household where he can work at the trade he wants to pursue. The move is supervised not only by his father but also by the magistrates, to make sure the master of his adoptive household is respectable and responsible. Actually, if someone has mastered one trade and wants to learn another besides, he gets permission to do so by the same procedure. When he has mastered both, he practices whichever he wants to, unless the city has a greater need for the other.[160]

The chief and practically the only function of the syphogrants is to take care and see to it that no one lounges around in idleness[161] but rather that everyone practices his trade diligently, but not working from early morning till late at night, exhausted by constant labor like a beast of burden.[162] For such grievous labor is fit only for slaves, and yet almost everywhere it is the way workmen live, except in Utopia.[163] Dividing the day and night into twenty-four equal hours, they devote only six to work, three before noon, when they go to lunch. After lunch they take two hours of rest in the afternoon, then three more given over to work, after which they have dinner. Counting the first hour after noon as ending at one o'clock, it is eight o'clock when they go to bed. Sleep takes up eight hours.

The intervals between work, meals, and sleep they are allowed to spend however they like, provided that the time they have free from work is not wasted in debauchery and idleness but spent well in some other pursuit, according to their preference. Many devote these intervals to intellectual activities. For every day they have regular lectures in the hours before dawn; attendance is required only from those who have been specially chosen to devote themselves to learning. But a great number of men, and also women, from all orders of society flock to hear these lectures, some one sort, some another, as each is naturally inclined. But if someone wishes to spend this same time practicing his trade (as do many whose temperaments are not suited to any abstract discipline), they are quite free to do so; indeed they are also praised for doing so, since their labor contributes to the common good.

After dinner they devote one hour to recreation, during the summer in the gardens, during the winter in the common rooms where they have their meals. There they either play music or entertain themselves with conversation. They do not so much as know about dice and other such pointless and pernicious games,[164] but they do play two games not unlike chess. In one of them numbers fight against each other, one taking over the other; in the other game virtues are lined up in a battlefront against the vices. This game shows very cleverly both how the vices fight among themselves but join forces against the virtues, and also which vices are opposed to which virtues, what forces they bring to bear openly, what instruments they use to attack indirectly, what defenses the virtues use to fend off the forces of the vices, how they evade their assaults, and finally by what methods one side or the other wins the victory.

But at this point, it is necessary to examine the matter in more detail to avoid making a mistake. If only six hours are devoted to work, you might think that there would necessarily be some shortage of supplies. But that is so far from being true that six hours is not only enough to produce abundantly all the necessities and comforts of life but is even more than enough. This you, too, will understand if you consider what a large part of the population in other countries live their lives in idleness. First, almost all the women do,[165] and they make up almost half the population. Or in places where the women work, the men take their place and lie around snoring. Add to that the huge idle crowd of priests and religious, as they are called.[166] Throw in all the rich, especially the landlords of estates who are commonly called gentlemen and nobles. Include with them their retainers, that rank cesspool of worthless swashbucklers. Add, finally, the strong and sturdy beggars who feign some disease as a pretext for their idleness. You will certainly find that it takes far fewer than you thought to produce everything that mortals use.[167]

Now consider how few of these workers are occupied in necessary trades, since, where money is the measure of everything, many completely futile and superfluous crafts must be practiced just to support over-indulgence and wanton luxury. Now if that same crowd who are presently working were divided up among the few trades needed to produce the few commodities that nature requires, the resulting abundance of goods would drive prices down so low that craftsmen could not make a living. But if all those who work away at pointless tasks and, together with them, that whole crowd of lazy, languid idlers (any single one of whom consumes twice as much as any of the workers who produce the goods), if they all were put to work—and useful work at that—you can easily see how little time would be enough and more than enough time to produce all the goods required for human needs and conveniences—and pleasures, too, as long as they are true and natural ones.

And this very point is confirmed by the experience of the Utopians. For there, in the whole city and the surrounding territory, out of all the men and women who are old enough and strong enough to work, barely five hundred are exempted from work.[168] Among them the syphogrants, who are legally relieved from work, nevertheless do not exempt themselves; they work so as to motivate others to work by giving a good example. The same immunity is enjoyed by those to whom the people give total leisure to pursue various branches of learning, but only after the priests have recommended them and the syphogrants have chosen them by a secret ballot. If any of them disappoints the hopes they had in him, he is put back to work; and on the other hand, it happens, not infrequently, that an artisan, devoting his free time to intellectual pursuits, works so diligently and makes such progress that he is exempted from working at his trade and promoted to the scholarly class. From this order of scholars are chosen ambassadors, priests, tranibors, and finally the ruler himself, who was called Barzanes in their ancient language, but is named Ademus in the modern tongue.[169] The remaining group, which is neither idle nor devoted to useless trades, is so large that it is easy to imagine how many goods they produce in so few hours.

Apart from what I have just said, they have it easier because in most of the necessary trades they do not need to expend as much labor as in other nations. First of all, building or repairing structures everywhere else requires the continuous effort of so many workers for the simple reason that what a father has built his worthless heir allows to fall gradually into disrepair. Thus what could have been maintained with a minimum of effort has to be totally rebuilt, at great expense, by the next heir. Moreover, it often happens that a house that cost someone enormous sums to build seems contemptible to someone of more fastidious taste; after a short time it falls into ruin through neglect and the owner builds another house somewhere else, at no less expense. But among the Utopians, from the time when everything was settled and the commonwealth was established, it very rarely happens that a new site is chosen on which to build houses; and they not only repair damage quickly when it happens but they take preventive measures against it. The result is that their buildings last a very long time and require very little work, and sometimes construction workers have so little to do that they are set to shaping timbers or squaring and fitting stones at home, so that if they ever need to build anything, it can be constructed more quickly.

Now as for their clothing, notice how little labor it requires. First of all, at work they wear informal garments made of leather or skins which last for seven years. When they go out in public they put on cloaks which cover these rough clothes; throughout the island they are all of the same color, that of the natural wool. Thus they not only get along with much less woolen cloth than anywhere else, but it also costs much less. But linen is easier to work and hence they use more of it; they are concerned only about the whiteness of linen and the neatness of wool, for they place no value on fineness of weave. The result is that in other places four or five woolen cloaks and the same number of silk shirts are not enough for one person, and if he is a bit fastidious, not even ten will do, but there everybody is content with one, which generally lasts for two years. Naturally there is no reason why he should want any more, for if he got them he would have no more protection against the cold, and his clothing would not look the least bit more fashionable.

Therefore, since everyone is employed in a useful trade and the trades themselves require less labor, the result is a great abundance of everything, so that sometimes they bring out an enormous number of people to repair the public roads, if any have deteriorated. It happens very often, when there is no occasion even for that kind of work, that they publicly decree a shorter workday. For the magistrates do not compel anyone to engage in superfluous labor against his will, since the structure of the commonwealth is primarily designed to relieve all the citizens from as much bodily labor as possible, so that they can devote their time to the freedom and cultivation of the mind. For that, they think, constitutes a happy life.

SOCIAL RELATIONS

Now is the time, I think, to explain how they treat each other, how they interact with one another, and what system they have for distributing goods.

And so, while the city is made up of households, the households themselves consist mostly of blood relatives. Girls, when they grow up and marry, move into the dwellings of their husbands. But sons and, after them, grandsons remain in the household and are subject to the oldest parent, unless his mind is failing because of old age; in that case he is replaced by the next oldest. But to keep the city from being either over- or underpopulated, they see to it that no household (and each city, apart from its territory, has six thousand of them) has fewer than ten or more than sixteen adults. For it is not possible to set a limit for children.[170] This limit is easily maintained by transferring persons from households with too many people to those with too few. But if it should happen that the whole city grows too large, they use the excess to supply underpopulated cities. But if it should happen that throughout the island the whole mass of the population should swell inordinately, they sign up citizens from each city and send them as colonists to live under their own laws on the nearest part of the continent, wherever the natives have a lot of land left over and uncultivated; they adopt any natives who choose to live with them. Assenting willingly to the same style of life and the same customs, the natives are easily assimilated, and that to the advantage of both groups. For by means of their institutions the Utopians make the land easily support both peoples, whereas before it provided a meager and skimpy living for only one. The natives who refuse to live under their laws are driven out of the territory the Utopians have marked off for their use; if they resist, the Utopians make war against them. For they think it is quite just to wage war against someone who has land which he himself does not use, leaving it fallow and unproductive, but denying its possession and use to someone else who has a right, by the law of nature, to be maintained by it.[171] If any of their cities is ever accidentally so reduced in population that they cannot replenish it from other parts of the island and still keep the full quota in those cities (which they say has only happened twice in their whole history because of a virulent plague), then they resupply it with citizens immigrating from a colony. For they would rather allow the colonies to disappear than let any of the cities on the island shrink in size.

But, to return to the citizens' way of life, the oldest man, as I said, presides over a household. Wives serve their husbands and children their parents, and generally the younger serve the older.[172] Each city is divided into four equal districts. In the middle of each district is a marketplace for all sorts of commodities. The products of each household are taken to designated houses there and each kind of goods is separately stored in a warehouse. From them each head of household goes to get whatever he and his household need, and he takes away whatever he wants, paying no money and giving absolutely nothing in exchange for it. For why should he be denied anything, since there is plenty of everything and no one need fear that anyone would want to ask for more than he needs? For why should anyone be suspected of asking for too much if he is certain he will never lack for anything? Certainly fear of want makes all kinds of animals greedy and rapacious, but only mankind is made so by pride, which makes them consider their own glory enhanced if they excel others in displaying superfluous possessions; in the Utopian scheme of things there is no place at all for such a vice.

Adjoining the marketplaces I mentioned are food markets, to which vegetables, fruit, and bread are brought, and also fish and edible birds and beasts are conveyed from designated places outside the city where there is a stream to wash away refuse and offal. From here they bring the cattle which have been slaughtered and cleaned by the hands of bondsmen. For they do not allow their own citizens to become accustomed to butchering animals; they think that to do so gradually eliminates compassion, the finest feeling of human nature. They do not allow anything filthy or foul to be brought into the city, for air tainted by such rottenness might engender disease.

Furthermore, each block has spacious halls located at equal intervals, each known by its own name. The syphogrants look after them, and to each of them are assigned thirty families (namely fifteen on either side) who eat their meals there.[173] Stewards from each hall gather in the market at a designated hour and get food according to the number of mouths they have to feed.

But their first priority is the sick, who are cared for in public hospitals. They have four of them on the outskirts of the city, a little outside the walls; they are as capacious as four little towns so that no matter how many people are sick they do not need to be crowded uncomfortably together, and so that those who have contagious diseases that can be transferred from one person to another can be kept at a distance from the main body of the patients. These hospitals are so equipped and provided with everything that promotes health, the care provided in them is so gentle and solicitous, the doctors who are in constant attendance are so skilled that, although no one is sent there against his will, there is still almost no one in the whole city who would not rather be lodged there than at home when he is in failing health.

After the stewards of the hospitals have received the food prescribed by the physicians, the best of what is left is divided equitably among the halls, according to the number fed by each one, except that they pay special attention to the ruler, the high priest, and the tranibors, and also to ambassadors and all foreigners (if there are any, for they are few and far between); but when there are any, designated residences are furnished and prepared for them. At the times fixed for lunch and dinner, the whole syphograncy, alerted by the blast of a bronze trumpet, convenes in these halls, except for those who are bedridden in the hospitals or at home. Nevertheless, no one is forbidden to take home food from the marketplace once the halls have been supplied with their quotas, for they know that no one would lightly choose to do so; though no one is prohibited from eating at home, still no one does it willingly, for it is not considered proper and it would be foolish to go to the trouble of preparing an inferior meal at home when a splendid and sumptuous one is ready and waiting in a hall nearby.[174]

In this hall slaves perform all the chores which are somewhat heavy or dirty. But the women are solely[175] responsible for preparing and cooking the food and making arrangements for the whole meal, each household taking its turn. They sit at three tables or more, according to the number of diners. The men sit with their backs to the wall, the women on the outside, so that if they should suddenly feel ill, as happens, sometimes, when they are pregnant, they can get up and go out to the nurses without disturbing the seating arrangement.

The nurses are seated separately with the nursing infants in a little room assigned to them; it never lacks a fire and clean water and also cradles so that when they want they can either lay them down or take off their swaddling clothes and let them refresh themselves by playing freely. Every mother nurses her own child unless death or disease prevents it. When that happens, the wives of the syphogrants immediately find a nurse, and that is not hard to do. For those who can are more than willing because everyone praises their compassion and the infant who is brought up this way takes the nurse as its natural mother.[176]

Children who are under five sit in the nurses' den. Other minors, among whom they include members of both sexes who are not yet old enough to marry, either serve the diners, or, if they are too young and not strong enough for that, stand by—and that in absolute silence. Both groups eat what is handed to them by those seated at table, nor is any other time set aside for them to eat.[177]

The syphogrant and his wife sit at the head table, which is the place of honor and overlooks the whole assembly, since it is placed crosswise in the highest part of the chamber. Next to them sit two of the oldest persons, for they sit in groups of four at all the tables. But if a church is located in that syphograncy, the priest and his wife sit with the syphogrant so as to preside.[178] On both sides of them sit younger people, and then older people again, and so on throughout the whole hall. And so people sit with their coevals, and yet they are mixed in with a different age group. They say that this arrangement was adopted so that the dignity of the elders and the respect due them would keep the young people from indulging in improper language or behavior, since nothing can be done or said at table which would escape the notice of the persons sitting nearby on all sides.

The dishes of food are not served to the highest places and then downward to the others, but rather the choicest pieces are served first to the old people (whose places are marked) and then equitable shares are served to the rest. But some of the delicacies which are not in sufficient supply to be distributed to the whole hall are given by the old people, as they see fit, to those sitting near them. Thus respect for the elders is maintained and yet everyone has the same advantage from it.

Lunch and dinner always begin with some reading that concerns morals, but it is brief lest it be tedious.[179] Taking off from this, the elders begin the discussion, but not in a gloomy and sour fashion. And they do not take up the whole meal with long disquisitions. No, they would much rather listen to the young people, and they even deliberately challenge them so as to learn about the temperament and intelligence of each of them as revealed in the free give and take of tabletalk.

Lunches are quite brief, dinners more ample because the one is followed by work and the other by rest and sleep during the night, which they think contribute more to good digestion.[180] They never dine without music and after dinner they never lack for tasty desserts. They light incense and sprinkle perfumes and spare no effort to cheer up the diners. For they tend to incline to the position that no kind of pleasure ought to be forbidden as long as no harm comes of it.

This is the way they live in the city. But in the country, since they live far apart, they all eat in their own homes. No household has any shortage of food, since, after all, everything eaten by the city-dwellers comes from the farmers.

HOW THE UTOPIANS TRAVEL

If someone wants to visit friends who live in another city or is simply taken with a desire to see the place, he easily gets the permission of his syphogrant and tranibor unless a necessary job keeps him from going. He is sent out as part of a group, with a letter from the ruler which grants them permission and sets the day they must be back. They are provided with a carriage and a public slave to drive the oxen and take care of them. But unless there are women in the group, they leave the carriage behind as more of a hindrance than a help. Throughout the whole journey they carry nothing with them; yet they lack for nothing and are at home everywhere. If they stay anywhere longer than one day, each of them works at his trade and is treated very kindly by his fellow craftsmen.

If someone takes it upon himself to wander outside his territory, when he is caught without the ruler's passport, he is treated with contempt, brought back as a runaway, and severely punished. If he dares to repeat the offense, he is punished with slavery. But if someone is taken with a longing to wander through the fields belonging to his own city, he is not prohibited from doing so, as long as he gets his father's permission and his wife's consent. But wherever he goes in the countryside, he is not given any food until he has done the work allotted to the morning or however much work is usually done there before dinner.[181] Under this regulation he is allowed to go anywhere within the boundaries of his city's territory, for he will be no less useful to the city than if he were in it.

So you see that nowhere is there any chance to be idle; there is no excuse for laziness, no wine taverns, no alehouses, no brothels, no occasion to be corrupted, no hideouts, no hangouts.[182] With the eyes of everyone upon them, they have no choice but to do their customary work or to enjoy pastimes which are not dishonorable. Such behavior on the part of the people is bound to produce an abundance of everything. And when it is distributed equitably to everyone, it follows that no one can be reduced to poverty or forced to beg.

In the senate at Amaurot (to which, as I said before, three representatives come every year from each city), once they have determined what surpluses are at hand in each place and what places have shortages, they immediately make up the deficiencies of the one with the excess supplies of the other, and they provide them as a free gift, receiving nothing in return from those to whom they gave them. But if they gave something to a city and received nothing in return, they also get what they need from some other city and pay nothing for it. Thus the whole island is like one household.

When they have enough provisions for themselves (which they do not think they do unless they have provided for two years, since the next year's outcome is uncertain), they export to other countries vast quantities of grain, honey, wool, linen, timber, red and purple dye, fleece, wax, tallow, leather, and also livestock. They give one-seventh of all this to the poor in that country and sell the rest at a moderate price. In exchange they not only acquire goods they do not have at home (they lack almost nothing except iron) but also they bring back to their homeland enormous quantities of silver and gold. They have continued this practice for such a long time that they now have everywhere a greater supply of those metals than you would think possible. Hence they do not much care whether they are paid in cash or credit, and they accept promissory notes for most of what is owed them, but never from private persons; instead they make the usual legal documents binding on the city government.[183] When the loan comes due, the city requires it to be paid by the private debtors and puts it in the public treasury; then the city enjoys the use of it until the Utopians call it in. For the most part they never do, since they think it is hardly right to claim what is of no use to them from those who have a use for it. But if circumstances require that they lend part of it to another nation they call it in, or when they are obliged to go to war; that is the only reason they keep all of the treasure which they have at home, as protection against extreme danger or sudden emergencies. They use it especially to pay enormous wages to foreign mercenaries, whom they would much rather expose to danger than their own citizens. They are also aware that with large sums of money even the enemies themselves can be bought and set against one another, either through treason or open hostilities.

This is the reason they reserve such an incalculable treasure, although they do not keep it as treasure but in a form I am really ashamed to tell you. I am afraid you will not believe what I say, and all the more rightly so since I am aware that if I had not seen it in person I would have been reluctant to believe it if someone else told it to me.[184] For in general the more foreign something is to the habits of the listeners, the harder it must be for them to believe it. But actually, a prudent judge of the matter will perhaps be less surprised that they handle silver and gold in their own way rather than ours, since all their arrangements are so different from ours. In fact, since they themselves have no use for money but rather keep it as protection against events which might or might not happen, in the meantime they keep gold and silver (from which money is made) in a form that lets no one place more value on it than it deserves by its nature. And obviously it deserves far less than iron, without which mortals could no more live, by heaven, than they could without fire or water, whereas nature gave to gold and silver no use which we could not easily do without; the folly of mankind gives them value because they are rare, but nature, on the other hand, like a kind and gracious mother, made the most useful elements openly available, like air, water, and earth, but she hid away what is vain and unprofitable in the most remote recesses.

Now if in their society these metals were put away in some tower, the ruler and the senate might be suspected of deceiving the people by some trick and getting some good from it for themselves—such is the foolish anxiety of the mob. And then if they made platters out of them or other vessels made by goldsmiths, if ever the occasion arose to melt them down and use them to pay mercenaries, they realize that once people had begun to delight in them they would be reluctant to give them up. To obviate these difficulties they have thought up a method quite compatible with the rest of their arrangements but very far removed from ours (for we value gold very highly and hide it away quite carefully), a method which is therefore hard to believe unless you have experienced it. Whereas they eat and drink from vessels of earthenware and glass, beautifully crafted but inexpensive, they use gold and silver, not only in the common halls but also in private houses, to make all the chamberpots and lowliest containers.[185] Moreover, the chains and heavy shackles used to restrain the slaves are made of the same metals. Finally, the most notorious criminals wear gold rings in their ears, gold rings on their fingers, a gold collar around their necks, and even a gold band around their heads. By these means they see to it that the same metals which other nations give up with almost as much grief as if their guts were being pulled out have so little value that if circumstances required the Utopians to part with all such metals none of them would think they had lost as much as a single farthing.

Furthermore, they gather pearls on the seashore and even diamonds and rubies on some cliffs; they do not look for them, however, but when they have found some by chance, they polish them. They use them to deck out their infants, who are boastful and proud of such gems in their earliest childhood; but, as they get a little older and notice that such trinkets are worn only by children, they become ashamed of them of their own accord and, with no urging from their parents, they give them up just as our children discard their baubles, necklaces, and dolls when they grow up.

These arrangements, so different from those of other peoples, have produced quite different feelings and attitudes. That never became clearer to me than in the incident of the Anemolian ambassadors.[186] They came to Amaurot while I was there and since they had come to discuss important matters, the three citizens chosen by every city had come before they arrived. All the ambassadors from neighboring countries, who had landed there before and were familiar with the customs of the Utopians, knew that they did not revere sumptuous clothing, considered silk contemptible, and even associated gold with disgrace; and so they used to come clothed as modestly as possible. But the Anemolians lived further away and had less contact with them. Hence, when they saw that all the Utopians wore one and the same rough garment, they thought they did so because they had nothing better to wear and, with more pride than wisdom, they decided to set themselves up as gods by the elegance of their trappings and to dazzle the eyes of the poor Utopians by the splendor of their garb.

And so when the three ambassadors made their entry, their retinue of a hundred retainers was dressed in particolored garments, mostly made of silk, but the ambassadors themselves, who were noblemen in their own country, were garbed in cloth of gold, with large chains and earrings of gold, and also golden rings on their fingers, and on top of that strings of pearls and gems hanging from their hats, and in sum, decked out in everything that the Utopians use to punish slaves, to mark off someone in disgrace, or to make toys for children. And so it was a sight to see how they ruffled their feathers when they compared their finery with the clothing of the Utopians (for the people had poured out onto the streets). On the other hand, it was no less delightful to observe how totally mistaken their hopes and expectations were and how far they were from the consideration they thought they would receive. For in the eyes of all the Utopians, except for the very few who had had some good reason to travel to foreign countries, all their splendid trappings seemed shameful. They greeted all the retainers of the lowest rank reverently as if they were lords. But they considered the ambassadors to be slaves because they wore golden chains, and so they passed over them with no respect whatever. In fact, you could have also seen children there who had thrown away their gems and pearls. When they saw such gems affixed to the hats of the ambassadors, they nudged their mothers and said: "Look, mother, that big lout is still wearing little pearls and gems, as if he were a little boy!" But the mother would reply in all seriousness: "Hush, my son, I think he is one of the ambassadors' fools."[187] Others criticized those golden chains as useless because they were so fine that a slave could easily break them and so loosely fastened that a slave could shake them off whenever he wanted and run off anywhere he wanted, footloose and fancy-free.

But after the ambassadors had lived there for a day or two and seen such an enormous amount of gold treated as if it were worthless and contemned there as much as it was honored in their countries, and when they also noticed that the chains and shackles of only one runaway slave contained more gold and silver than the trappings of all three of them, they were crestfallen and sheepishly put away all the finery which they had so haughtily displayed, especially after they had talked more informally with the Utopians and learned their customs and opinions.

Indeed they are amazed that any mortal can take delight in the dubious[188] sparkle of a tiny gem or precious stone when he can look at a star or even at the sun, or how anyone could be so insane as to imagine that he is nobler because of fine-spun woolen thread, since that wool (however fine-spun) was once worn by a sheep, which was at the same time nothing more than a sheep.[189] They are likewise amazed that gold, which in itself is useless, is now prized so highly everywhere that mankind itself, which gave it value and for whose use it got that value, is valued much less than the gold itself, so much so that some beef-witted blockhead, who has morals to match his folly, nevertheless has many wise and good men in his service, for no better reason than that he has a heap of gold coins.[190] And if some turn of Fortune or trick of the law (which turns things topsy-turvy no less than Fortune herself) should transfer this heap from the heir to the lowest lout in the whole household, the master would shortly enter the service of his servant as if he were a mere adjunct and appendage of the coins. But what they find most amazing and despicable is the insanity of those who all but worship the rich, to whom they owe nothing and who can do them no harm; they do so for no other reason except that they are rich, knowing full well that they are so mean and tightfisted that they will certainly never give them one red cent during their whole lives.[191]

These opinions and others like them they have formed partly from their upbringing, since they were brought up in a commonwealth whose institutions are farthest removed from those kinds of folly, and partly from instruction and books. For though not many in each city are dispensed from physical labor and assigned to do nothing but study (namely those in whom they have perceived from their childhood remarkable talent, extraordinary intelligence, and devotion to learning), nevertheless all children are introduced to good books, and throughout their lives a good many people, both men and women, devote to learning the hours I have mentioned as free from labor.

They learn the various branches of knowledge in their own language, which has no lack of vocabulary, is not unpleasant to the ear, and is not surpassed by any other in the expression of thought. It has spread throughout most of that part of the world, though everywhere else it is corrupted in various ways.

Of all the philosophers[192] whose names are so famous in

this known part of the world, they had not so much as heard of any before our arrival, and yet in music, dialectic, arithmetic, and geometry,[193] they have made almost the same discoveries as our own ancient writers did. But though they measure up to our ancient writers in almost all respects, they are not up to the discoveries of modern dialecticians.[194] In fact, they have not discovered a single one of those rules about restrictions, amplifications, and suppositions which have been so subtly excogitated in the *Parva logicalia* and which are taught to young men everywhere in our world.[195] And then, as for second intentions,[196] they are so far from being able to understand them that none of the Utopians could see man in general,[197] as they say, even when we pointed him out with our finger, though, as you know, he is plainly colossal and bigger than any giant. But they are very expert in the orbits of stars and the movement of heavenly bodies. In fact, they have devised instruments of various designs which enable them to understand very accurately the movements and positions of the sun and moon and also the other stars which are visible in their hemisphere. But as for the conjunctions and oppositions of the planets and the whole fraud of divination by the stars, they have never so much as dreamed of it.[198] By means of signs that they have perceived from long observation they predict rainstorms, winds, and other changes in the weather. But concerning the causes of those phenomena, and concerning tides and the saltiness of the ocean, and in general concerning the origin and nature of the heavens and the world, they agree on some points with our own ancient philosophers, and on others, just as the ancients disagreed with one another, they also differ from all the ancients and propose new theories, and yet they do not entirely agree among themselves.[199]

In that area of philosophy which deals with ethics, they discuss the same issues as we do. They inquire about the goods of the mind and body and external goods, and whether the designation "good" applies to all of these or only to the gifts of the mind.[200] They discuss virtue and pleasure, but the primary and principal controversy is about what they think human happiness consists in, whether one thing or many. On this point they seem over-inclined to the position which claims that all or the most important part of human happiness consists of pleasure.[201] And what is even more surprising, they claim support for this self-indulgent view even from religion, which is sober and strict and, indeed, almost gloomy and stern. For they never analyze happiness unless they combine some religious principles with the rational analysis of philosophy, since they think that without such principles reason by itself is too weak and deficient to investigate true happiness.[202]

These principles are of this sort:[203] that the soul is immortal, and by the beneficence of God is born for happiness; that our virtues and good deeds will be rewarded after this life, and our crimes have punishments prepared for them.[204] Though these are religious principles, the Utopians still think that reason leads them to believe and grant them; if they are eliminated, the Utopians have no hesitation in affirming that no one could be so stupid as not to feel that he ought to pursue his own pleasure by hook or crook. He would only be concerned not to sacrifice a greater pleasure for a lesser one and not to pursue one that would be requited by pain. For they think it would be truly insane to pursue virtue, which is harsh and difficult, and not only to banish the pleasures of life but even to seek out pain of your own accord, and to expect to get nothing out of it (for how can you get anything out of it if you get nothing after death, since you have spent your whole life here without pleasure, that is, wretchedly?). But as it is, they think happiness consists not in every sort of pleasure but in pleasure that is good and honorable, for they believe that our nature is drawn to pleasure as the highest good by virtue itself, whereas the opposite faction attributes happiness to virtue alone.[205]

And then they define virtue as living according to nature; to that end, they say, we were created by God.[206] We follow the guidance of nature when we obey reason in choosing and avoiding things. Furthermore, reason above all inspires mortals to love and revere the majesty of God, to whom we owe our very existence and our capacity to be happy. Secondly, reason admonishes and encourages us to lead lives with as little anxiety and as much joy as possible and, beyond that, to exert ourselves in helping all others achieve the same end because of our natural fellowship. For not even the gloomiest and sternest advocate of virtue, who despises pleasure so much that he would impose toil, vigils, and mortifications on you, would refrain from enjoining you to do as much as you can to alleviate the poverty and distress of others, and he would think it praiseworthy and humane for one human being to rescue and comfort another, since the very essence of humanity (and no virtue is more proper to human beings) is to relieve the distress of others, eliminate sadness from their lives, and restore them to a joyful life, that is, to pleasure. Why should nature not impel us to do the same for ourselves? For either a joyful life, that is, a life of pleasure, is wrong and in that case we should not only not help anyone to achieve it but rather we should do all we can to make everyone avoid it as harmful and deadly, or if you are not only allowed but even required to obtain it for others, why not do so first of all for yourself? You should be no less well-disposed to yourself than to others. For when nature prompts you to be good to others, she does not require you to turn around and be cruel and merciless to yourself. Nature herself, they say, prescribes as the aim of all our actions a joyful life, that is, pleasure, and they define virtue as following the prescriptions of nature.[207] But when nature invites mortals to help each other to lead cheerful lives (and she is certainly right to do so, since no one is so far above the rank of human beings that nature should care for him alone, whereas in fact she is equally concerned about all those whom she groups together as belonging to the same species), she also, of course, forbids you time after time to seek your own advantages in ways that create disadvantages for others.

Therefore they think that not only private agreements must be kept but also public laws which have either been promulgated by a good ruler or which a people not oppressed by a tyrant or deceived by some trick have laid down by common consent to govern the distribution of vital commodities, that is, the means to pleasure. As long as these laws are not broken, to look out for your own good is prudent; to promote the public good is pious. But to deprive someone else of pleasure to promote your own is wrong; on the other hand, to deprive yourself of something to give it to someone else is a work of humanity and kindness and it always brings you more good than it takes away. For it is counterbalanced by gifts given in return, and also your consciousness of having done a good deed and the thought of the love and good will of those you have benefited will give you mental pleasure that outweighs any loss of bodily comfort. Finally, as religion makes clear to true believers, God will repay the loss of brief and paltry pleasures with

enormous and never-ending joy. Following this line of reasoning and having considered the matter long and hard, they
think that all our actions, including also our virtuous deeds,
are directed toward pleasure as our happiness and final end.[208]

They define pleasure as any motion or state of the mind or
body which produces delight in accord with the guidance of
nature. Not without reason do they add that the impulse must
be in accord with nature. For just as not only our senses but
also our reason pursues whatever is pleasurable by nature, that
is, pleasures not achieved through wrongdoing, or acquired
with the loss of a greater pleasure, or followed by hardship, so
too they hold that all those unnatural pleasures which mortals
agree to call delightful by the emptiest of fictions (as if it were
in their power to change the thing by changing the name) are
so far from contributing to happiness that they actually hinder
it because, once they have taken over the mind, they occupy it
totally and leave no room for true and genuine pleasures. For a
great many things are not pleasurable by their very nature and
are, in fact, for the most part bitter, but through the perverse
enticement of evil desires they are not only thought to be the
greatest pleasures but are even included among the primary
reasons for living.

Among those who pursue false pleasures they include those
whom I mentioned before who think that the finer the gown
they wear the better they are. On this one point they are wrong
twice over. They are no less deceived in thinking the gown is
better than in imagining they themselves are. For if you consider the usefulness of a garment, why is wool woven with fine
thread better than wool woven with coarser thread? But they
think they excel in fact, not merely in their illusions. They
ruffle their feathers; they believe that they are more valuable

because of their clothes. And on that basis, honors they would not have dared hope for in cheaper clothes they demand as rightly due to their elegant gown, and they are outraged if someone passes them by without due deference.

And then isn't it equally stupid to be much taken with empty and worthless honors? For what natural pleasure is there in someone's baring his head to you or bending his knee? Will that relieve the pain in your own knee or cure the delirium in your head? It is amazing how some are caught up in this imaginary, specious pleasure: delightfully insane, they flatter themselves and take pride in their imagined nobility simply because they happen to be descended from a long series of ancestors who are considered to be rich, above all rich landlords (for nowadays there is no other source of nobility except wealth), and yet they think they are not a whit the less noble even if their ancestors have left them no wealth or they themselves have squandered it.

With these they group the persons I mentioned before who are enthralled by gems and precious stones and almost think they have been deified if they ever get a fine specimen, especially if it is the sort most highly valued in their own times; for not all sorts are highly regarded by all persons and at all times. But they do not buy such a stone unless it is removed from its gold setting and exposed, and even then not unless the seller swears and guarantees that it is a genuine jewel and a true gemstone; so afraid are they that their eyes may be deceived by a counterfeit substituted for a real stone. For why should your eyes be any less delighted by a counterfeit since they cannot distinguish it from a real one? To you each of them should have equal value, no less so, by heaven, than they would to a blind man.

What about people who keep superfluous wealth under lock and key, taking delight not in using the amassed treasure but merely in contemplating it? Do they feel any real delight or rather are they not deluded by a false pleasure? How about those who are subject to a different vice and hide away their gold, intending not only never to use it but perhaps never even to see it any more; in their anxiety not to lose it, they lose it. For surely it is lost if it is buried in the ground so as to be of no use to you and perhaps not to any other mortal. But still, when the treasure is hidden away, you feel carefree and happy. If a thief took it away and you died ten years later without knowing of the theft, in all those years that you lived after the money was stolen, what difference did it make to you whether it was removed or remained safe?[209] In either case its usefulness to you was the same.

To these categories of absurd enjoyment they add gambling (a sort of madness they know of only through hearsay, not experience) and also hunting and falconry. For what pleasure can there be, they say, in throwing dice on a gaming table? Even if there were any pleasure in it, you have done it so often that mere repetition should have made you sick of it. How can it be delightful to hear the barking and howling of dogs?—isn't that a disgusting noise? Why do hunters feel more pleasure when a dog chases a hare than when a dog chases a dog?[210] For in either case the action is the same, that is, running, if that is what pleases you. Or if you are attracted by the hope of carnage and the expectation of seeing the slaughter with your own eyes, you ought instead to be moved to compassion when you see a little hare torn to pieces by a dog, a weak creature tormented by a stronger one, a timid creature fleeing from a ferocious beast, a harmless creature from a cruel hound. And so the Utopians have assigned the whole business of hunting to the butchers, whose trade (as I said before) is conducted entirely by slaves, considering it beneath the dignity of free men.[211] They consider it the lowest function of the trade. The other activities of butchers are more useful and honorable, since they contribute much more and destroy animals only out of necessity, whereas the hunter seeks nothing but pleasure from the slaughter and butchering of some poor little creature. Even in beasts themselves,[212] according to the Utopians, such an eagerness to view carnage springs from a cruel disposition, or else the continual indulgence in such brutal pleasure finally degenerates into cruelty.

Though the herd of mortals consider such pursuits as these and others like them (for there is no end to them) to be pleasures, the Utopians firmly hold that they have nothing to do with pleasure, since there is no natural sweetness in them. Though they ordinarily produce sensual joy (which seems to be the function of pleasure), the Utopians are unwilling to change their minds. The reason they seem pleasant is not the nature of the things themselves but the perverse habits of their devotees, whose vicious attitudes cause them to embrace what is bitter as sweet, just as the defective tastebuds of pregnant women make them think that pitch and tallow are sweeter than honey. And yet no one's judgment, if it is vitiated by disease or habit, can change the nature of pleasure, or of anything else for that matter.

True pleasures they divide into various classes, assigning some to the mind, others to the body. To the mind they attribute understanding and the sweetness which springs from the contemplation of the truth. To these they add the pleasure of looking back on a lifetime of good deeds and the sure hope of happiness to come.

They divide bodily pleasure into two kinds: one is the sweetness which pervades the senses, either when the supplies our natural heat has used up are replenished (as they are by food and drink) or else when the excessive elements overburdening our bodies are discharged. This happens when we purge our intestines of excrement, or go about generating children or when the itching in some part of the body is alleviated by rubbing or scratching. But sometimes pleasure results not from the replenishment sought by our bodily members nor from relieving them of excess but from some secret but remarkable power which tickles, excites, and attracts our senses to itself, such as the pleasure arising from music.

They claim that there is another kind of bodily pleasure which consists in the balanced and quiet condition of the body, that is, when a person's health is not disturbed by any disease. Such health, as long as it is not interrupted by any pain, is delightful in itself, even though it is not affected by any external pleasure. Though it is less obvious and affects the senses less grossly than the insistent desire for food and drink, nevertheless many Utopians hold it to be the greatest pleasure of all. Almost all of them believe that it is a great pleasure and the foundation and basis, as it were, of all the others, since it is the only one which keeps our lives peaceful and desirable; and, if you take it away, there is no room left for any pleasure at all. For the mere absence of pain without health they regard as insensibility, certainly not as pleasure.

They have long since rejected the position of those who think that stable and undisturbed health should not be considered to be a pleasure because, they say, its presence can be felt only through some external stimulus (for they, too, have debated this question intensely). But now they are in almost complete agreement with the opposite position, that health is actually essential to pleasure. For according to them, disease brings pain, which is unalterably opposed to pleasure, in the same way as disease is opposed to health. Why not conclude, in turn, that there is pleasure in undisturbed health? On this point they do not think it makes any difference whether the disease is a pain or the pain comes from the disease; in either case the effect is the same. Thus, if health itself is a pleasure or if it necessarily brings pleasure with it as fire brings heat, the result in either case is that, wherever health is, stable pleasure cannot be lacking.

Moreover, when we eat, they say, what happens is that health, which has begun to fail, now has food as its ally in the battle against hunger. As it gradually becomes stronger, the very progress toward its ordinary vigor brings with it the pleasure of being reinvigorated. And so if health finds joy in the struggle, will it not rejoice when the victory is won? But when it has at last happily recovered its former strength, which was the sole object of the whole struggle, will it immediately become insensible and fail to recognize and embrace its own good? The idea that health is not perceived they consider to be very far from the truth. For when we are awake, who does not perceive that he is healthy—except someone who is not? Who can be so constricted by dullness and lethargy that he does not admit that health is delightful and enjoyable? And what is enjoyment but another name for pleasure?

Above all they embrace the pleasures of the mind, which they consider the first and foremost of all pleasures. They think that mental pleasure springs primarily from the practice of the virtues and the consciousness of a good life. Of the pleasures supplied by the body they give the first place to health. As for the pleasure of eating and drink and whatever else falls under a similar category of delight, they think they should be sought, but only for the sake of health, for such activities are not enjoyable in themselves but only insofar as they counter the unnoticed encroachments of ill health. And therefore a wise man, they say, should ward off disease rather than seek medicine for it and avoid pain rather than seek relief from it; just so it would be better not to have any need for such pleasure than to be relieved by it.

If anyone thinks that this kind of pleasure makes him happy, he must also confess that his life would be the happiest of all if it could be spent in perpetual hunger, thirst, and itching, followed by eating, drinking, scratching, and rubbing—and who can fail to see that such a life would be not only foul but also miserable? Certainly these are the lowliest of all pleasures, since they are the least unadulterated and never occur except in conjunction with the pain contrary to them. Thus the pleasure of eating is coupled with hunger, and not in equal proportions, for the pain is both longer and more intense. For it begins before the pleasure and never departs until the pleasure also ceases. Therefore they do not place much stock in such pleasures, except insofar as necessity demands them. But they also rejoice in them and gratefully acknowledge the kindness of Mother Nature, who uses the sweetest pleasures to entice her offspring to do what they must always be doing out of necessity. How irksome our lives would be if the daily ailments of hunger and thirst had to be warded off by drugs and bitter medications like the other diseases which afflict us less often?

They gladly cherish beauty, strength, agility as special and enjoyable gifts of nature. Certainly the pleasures which are mediated by our ears, eyes, and noses and which nature assigned as proper and peculiar to the human race (for no other kind of creature admires the design and beauty of the world, or is moved by the beauty of fragrances except to distinguish kinds of food, or recognizes the harmonious or discordant intervals in sounds), these pleasures, I say, they cultivate as adding a certain enjoyable spice to their lives. In all of them, however, they impose the limitation that a lesser should not impede a greater pleasure or that a pleasure should not cause pain at some later time—and they think this will necessarily happen if the pleasure is dishonorable.

They think it is certainly quite mad for someone to despise a beautiful figure, to deplete his strength, to turn agility into torpor, to wear out his body with fasting, to ruin his health, and to scorn the other favors bestowed by nature, unless he neglects his own good so as to work more avidly for the good of others or the public welfare, and in return for his effort he expects greater pleasure from God. Otherwise to inflict pain on oneself without doing anyone any good—simply to gain the empty shadow of virtue or to be able to bear with less distress adversities that may never come—this they consider to be insane and the mark of a mind that is both cruel to itself and ungrateful to nature, rejecting her benefits and not deigning to be beholden to her.

This is their view of virtue and pleasure; and in the absence of religious inspiration from heaven revealing something holier, they think human reason can discover no truer doctrine.[213] I do not have time now to examine whether or not their teaching is correct, nor is it necessary, since I undertook to present their principles, not to defend them. But whatever validity their precepts may have, I am fully persuaded that nowhere will you find a more extraordinary people or a happier commonwealth.

Physically they are agile and vigorous, stronger than you would expect from their height, though they are not under-sized. Though their soil is not uniformly fertile and their weather is not particularly favorable, they protect themselves from the climate by moderation in their diet and they work hard to remedy the defects of the soil, so that nowhere in the world will you find a more abundant supply of crops and cattle or bodies more vigorous and subject to fewer diseases. You can see them there diligently employing the usual agricultural methods of improving infertile soil by skill and effort, but you could also see a forest that they uprooted with their own hands and planted in another place. The reason for doing this was not greater production but transportation: they wanted the timber closer to the sea or rivers or the cities themselves, since it takes less labor to move crops by land over long distances than it does to transport timber.

They are an easy-going people, cheerful and clever. They enjoy their leisure but they endure physical labor well enough as long as it is useful (but otherwise they are hardly fond of it); in intellectual pursuits they are indefatigable. When we told them about the literature and learning of the Greeks (for in Latin there is nothing except the poets and historians that would be likely to interest them very much) it was amazing how eagerly they pressed us to help them master Greek by giving them instruction. And so we began to read, at first more out of a desire not to seem lazy than from any hope that much

good would come of it. But when we had made a little progress, their diligence immediately made us anticipate that ours
would not be wasted.[214] They began to imitate the shape of
the letters so easily, to pronounce the words so readily, to
memorize so quickly, and to recite so accurately that we would
have thought it miraculous except that the majority of them
had undertaken this study not only on their own initiative but
also at the explicit command of the senate, and hence they
were selected from the most talented and mature scholars.
And so in less than three years there was nothing in that
language which they had not mastered; they read good authors
with no hesitation, unless they encountered some textual crux.
I tend to think they mastered Greek all the more easily because
it is somewhat related to their own language. I suspect that the
Utopian people originally sprang from the Greeks because
their language, which is otherwise closest to Persian, preserves
some vestiges of Greek in the names of cities and magistrates.

On the fourth voyage, instead of trade goods I took on
board a fair-sized packet of books because I was fully determined to return only after a long time, if ever. From me they
got most of Plato's works, more of Aristotle's, and also Theo-
phrastus[215] *On Plants,* which was mutilated in several places,
I'm sorry to say. During the voyage the book had not been put
away properly and a playful monkey came upon it; he mis-
chievously ripped out some pages here and there and tore
them up. Of the grammarians they have only Lascaris, for I
did not take Theodore with me nor any dictionary except
Hesychius and Dioscorides.[216] They are very fond of Plutarch's
books and they are also much taken with the wit and elegance
of Lucian.[217] Of the poets they have Aristophanes, Homer,

93

and Euripides, and also Sophocles in the small typeface of Aldus.[218] Of the historians they have Thucydides and Herodotus, as well as Herodian.[219]

Furthermore, as for medical books, my companion Tricius Apinatus[220] had brought with him some shorter works of Hippocrates and the *Microtechne* of Galen;[221] for these books they have a high regard. Even though there is hardly a country in the world that has less need of medicine, still it is nowhere more honored, precisely because they consider a knowledge of it as one of the finest and most useful branches of science. When they investigate the secrets of nature using the resources of science, they not only experience wonderful pleasure from doing so but they also think they win the highest approbation from the creator and maker of the world. For they suppose that he, like other workmen, set up the marvelous mechanism of this world for mankind to view and contemplate (and men are the only creatures he made capable of doing so) and that therefore he is fonder of a careful observer and meticulous admirer than he is of some lazy blockhead who ignores such a marvelous spectacle as if he were a mindless brute.

And so the natural talent of the Utopians, trained by study, is marvelously effective in inventing techniques which make some contribution to a comfortable life. Two of these they owe to us, printing and papermaking, but even these they owe not only to us but in large part to themselves. For when we had shown them some books printed by Aldus on paper and had spoken a bit about the material for making paper and the technique of printing letters, though we did not really explain it (since none of us was expert in either process), they immediately and most ingeniously figured it out. And whereas before they had written only on vellum, bark, and papyrus, they immediately tried to make paper and to print with type. Though at first they did not get it quite right, by frequent attempts they soon mastered both techniques, and they became so proficient that if they had copies of Greek texts, there could have been no lack of printed editions. But as it is, they have no more than what I have mentioned, but what they have they have disseminated in many thousands of printed copies.

Any sightseers who visit them are especially welcome if they are recommended by unusual intellectual gifts or knowledge of many lands gained by traveling widely (and for that reason they welcomed us warmly when we landed), for they are eager to learn what is happening everywhere in the world. But not very many come there to trade. For what can they bring except iron or gold and silver, which they would prefer to take home than to export? As for their own exports, they think it more advantageous to deliver them themselves than to have others pick them up, for in that way they learn more about foreign countries everywhere and they keep their seamanship and nautical skills from getting rusty.

SLAVES

Prisoners of war they do not consider to be slaves except those captured in wars they themselves have fought.[222] The children of slaves and the slaves of foreign countries whom they have obtained are not kept in slavery.[223] Their slaves are those who have committed a serious crime in Utopia or foreigners who have been condemned to death for committing some crime (and these are by far the larger number), for the Utopians acquire many of them, sometimes cheaply, more often gratis, and take them away. These kinds of slaves they not only keep constantly at work but also in chains. Utopian slaves, however, they treat more harshly since they consider them baser and deserving of more severe punishment because they had an extraordinary education and the best of moral training, yet still could not be restrained from wrongdoing. Another class of slaves is made up of poor, overworked drudges from other nations who choose of their own accord to be slaves among the Utopians. These they treat decently and, except that they make them work a bit harder (since they are used to it), they are treated not much less kindly than the citizens. If they wish to depart (and that does not happen very often), they are not kept against their will nor are they sent away empty-handed.

They care for the sick, as I said, with great concern, omitting nothing whatever in the way of medicine or diet that might restore them to health. They sit with those who are suffering from an incurable disease, talk with them, console them, and do what they can to alleviate their pain. But if someone suffers from a disease which is not only incurable but also constantly and excruciatingly painful, then the priests and the magistrates point out that he can no longer live a useful life, that he is a heavy burden to himself and to others, and that he has outlived his own death; they encourage him to make a decision not to maintain the sickness and disease any longer and urge him not to hesitate to die, but rather to rely on hope for a better life; since he lives in a prison where he is cruelly tormented on the rack, he should escape from this miserable life on his own or willingly allow others to rescue him from it. This would be a wise act, they say, since death would deprive him of no advantages but would save him from suffering; and since in doing so he would be following the advice of the priests, the interpreters of God's will, it would also be a pious and holy deed.[224]

Those who agree with these arguments voluntarily starve themselves to death or are put to sleep and dispatched with no sensation of dying. But they do not do away with anyone who is unwilling, and they do not in any way diminish their attendance on him. Those who are persuaded and die in this way are treated with honor; but otherwise anyone who commits suicide for reasons not approved by the priests and senate is deemed unworthy of either burial or cremation and is ignominiously thrown into a swamp without a proper funeral.

A woman does not marry until she is eighteen, a man not until he is four years older than that.[225] If a man and a woman are convicted of engaging in secret intercourse before marriage, they are both severely reprimanded and they are forbidden ever to marry anyone unless the ruler remits the sentence. But both the master and the mistress of the household where the offense was committed fall into utter disgrace for not doing their duty with sufficient diligence. They punish this offense so severely because they foresee that few would join together in married love, living their whole lives with one person and enduring besides the troubles that come with marriage, if they were not carefully restrained from promiscuous intercourse.

Moreover, in choosing spouses they have a custom which seemed to us absolutely absurd and thoroughly ridiculous, but they observe it strictly and seriously. The bride, whether virgin or widow, is presented naked to the groom by a sober and respected matron, and the groom in turn is shown naked to the bride by some honorable man.[226] When we laughed at this custom and criticized it as ridiculous, they in turn were amazed at the extraordinary folly of all other nations: when they are buying a colt—a matter of no great expense—they are so cautious that even if the animal is almost completely exposed they refuse to buy it unless the saddle and saddlecloth are removed so as to reveal any sores that might be hidden beneath them; yet in choosing a spouse—a matter which will make them either happy or miserable for the rest of their lives—they are so careless that they judge her whole person by a mere handsbreadth, that is, by her face only, since the rest of her is wrapped up in her clothes, and according to that judgment they join themselves to her, not without great danger of not getting along with her if they later find something offensive. For not everyone is so wise as to pay attention only to character, and even in the marriages of the wise the gifts of the body add something to the virtues of the mind. Certainly some ugly deformity concealed beneath clothing can completely alienate a man's mind from his wife when his body can no longer be separated from her. If such a deformity should occur after the wedding, then everyone must put up with his lot; but before the wedding the laws should see to it that no one is duped or deceived.

All the more care needs to be taken because, of all the countries in that part of the world, they are the only one that is monogamous, and their marriages are almost never dissolved except by death, though adultery or unbearably offensive conduct can be grounds for divorce.[227] The offended party gets permission from the senate to remarry; the offender is disgraced and can never remarry. Otherwise, it is absolutely forbidden to put away a wife against her will and without any blame on her part because of some bodily disfigurement. They consider it cruel to desert someone at the very time she is in most need of comfort and they think it would make her uncertain and insecure about her old age, which brings diseases with it and is itself a disease.[228]

But sometimes it happens that two people are temperamentally incompatible, and if they have each found someone else with whom they hope they can live more agreeably, they separate by mutual consent and remarry, but not, however, without the permission of the senate, which does not permit divorce unless the senators and their wives have examined the case very carefully. Even then they do not do it readily because they know that the expectation of easily remarrying is hardly a means of strengthening the love of married couples.

Adulterers are punished with the harshest servitude, and if both were married the injured parties may divorce their spouses and marry each other if they wish to; otherwise they may marry whomever they like. But if one of the injured parties continues to love such an undeserving spouse, the marriage can remain intact, as long as the innocent party is willing to accompany the criminal condemned to hard labor; and it happens sometimes that the affectionate concern of the one and the repentance of the other move the ruler to mercy so that he sets them free again. But if the crime is repeated, it is punished with death.

Their laws do not prescribe punishments for other crimes, but rather the senate determines penalties according to how heinous or venial each particular offense seems to be. Husbands chastise their wives and parents their children, unless an offense is so serious that open punishment is advisable in order to maintain public morality. But generally the most serious crimes are punished with servitude, which they consider no less grievous to the criminal and much more advantageous to

the commonwealth than to execute wrongdoers and immediately get rid of them altogether. They do more good by their
labor than by their death, and they offer a long-standing example to deter others from similar crimes. If slaves are re-
bellious and unruly, then they are finally slaughtered like wild
beasts that cannot be restrained by bars or chains. But if they
are patient, they are not left entirely without hope. If they are
tamed by long suffering and show that they regret the sin more
than the punishment, their servitude may be either mitigated
or revoked, sometimes by the ruler's prerogative, sometimes by
popular vote.

Attempted seduction is no less dangerous than seduction
itself. In fact, in all sorts of crimes, they equate the clear and
deliberate attempt with the completed deed, for they do not
think that the mere incompletion of the deed should benefit
someone who did everything he could to complete it.

They are very fond of fools: they consider it quite shameful
to treat them with contempt, and they have nothing against
finding enjoyment in their foolery,[229] since they think that will
do the most good for the fools themselves. If anyone is so strict
and gloomy that he never laughs at any word or deed, they do
not entrust fools to him, out of fear that he would not treat
them kindly enough, since to him they would be not only
useless but not even entertaining—and that is the only talent
they have.

To mock someone for being disfigured or crippled is considered shameful and disfiguring, not to the person mocked
but to the mocker, since it is stupid for him to blame someone
for a defect which it is not in his power to avoid.

They consider it lazy and negligent not to keep up natural
beauty by grooming, but they consider seeking help from cos-

metics a disgraceful affectation. They know from experience itself that no physical beauty recommends wives to their husbands as much as respect and an upright character. Some men may be snared by beauty alone, but none can be held except by virtue and compliance.

They not only deter from crime by punishments, but they also foster virtue by rewarding it with honors. And so in the marketplace they set up statues of outstanding men who have done extraordinary service to the commonwealth, thus preserving the memory of their good deeds so that posterity may have the glory of their ancestors as a spur and incentive to virtuous deeds.

Anyone who campaigns for public office becomes disqualified for holding any office at all. The Utopians live together amiably, since no magistrate is arrogant or terrifying; they are called fathers and they live up to the name. Honor is willingly paid to them (as is proper); it is not exacted from those unwilling to give it. The ruler is not singled out by his clothes or a crown but rather by the sheaf of grain he carries: the sign of the high priest is a wax candle borne before him.

They have very few laws, for very few suffice for persons trained as they are. Indeed, one of their primary charges against other nations is that endless volumes of laws and interpretations are not sufficient. But they consider it quite unjust to bind people by laws which are so numerous no one can read through all of them or so obscure that no one can understand them. Moreover, they ban absolutely all lawyers as clever practitioners and sly interpreters of the law.[230] For they think it is practical that everyone should handle his own case and present the facts to the judge as he would to a lawyer; in this way there will be less confusion and the truth will be easier to determine, since he tells his story without having learned any evasion from a lawyer, while the judge weighs all the details carefully and protects simple souls from the false accusations of crafty litigants. In other countries, such straightforwardness is difficult to obtain because there is a mass of incredibly intricate laws. But among them everyone is knowledgeable about the laws. For, as I said, there are very few laws, and as for interpretations, they consider the most obvious the most correct. For though all laws (they say) are promulgated to inform everyone of his duty, a subtle interpretation will inform very few (for few can understand it); on the other hand, the simpler and more obvious meaning of the laws is clear to everyone. Otherwise, as far as ordinary people are concerned (and they constitute the largest group that needs to be informed), it would make no difference if you formulated no laws at all or if, after you have formulated them, you interpret them in such a way that no one can understand them without great intelligence and long analysis. The dull judgment of ordinary people is not adequate to that task, and they do not have enough time, occupied as they are in making a living.

Inspired by the virtues of the Utopians, those of their neighbors who are free and can choose as they please (for the Utopians themselves have long since liberated many of them from tyranny) ask for and obtain Utopians to act as their magistrates, some for a year, some for five years; when they have served their term, they bring them back to Utopia with great honor and praise, and take replacements with them back to their own country. And certainly these countries are providing very well and very effectively for the public welfare, which depends, for good or bad, on the character of the magistrates. What persons could they choose more wisely than those whose honesty cannot be undermined by bribes (since they will soon return to a place where money is useless) and who cannot be swayed by some person or faction, since they have no connections among that people? Wherever these two vices, favoritism and greed, get a hold on judicial decisions, all justice, which is the mainstay of the commonwealth, is immediately undermined. The peoples who recruit magistrates from them are called allies by the Utopians; the others on whom they have bestowed benefits are called friends.

They do not make treaties with any nation—such treaties as other nations so often make, break, and remake. What good is a treaty, they say, as if nature did not sufficiently bind one human being to another? And if someone scorns nature, do you think he will be concerned with mere words? They are especially drawn to that view because in that part of the world treaties and agreements between princes are not usually observed with very much good faith.

In Europe, of course, and especially in those parts which follow the faith and religion of Christ, the authority of treaties is everywhere holy and inviolable, partly because of the goodness and justice of the princes themselves, partly out of reverence and respect for the popes, who themselves undertake nothing which they do not carry out most scrupulously and likewise command all princes to keep their promises to the letter; if any prince reneges, the pope makes him comply by pastoral censure and sharp reproof.[231] Certainly they are right in thinking that it is quite shameful for those who are specifically called the faithful not to be faithful to their treaties.

But in that new world, which is as far from us in customs and way of life as it is removed from us by the distance the equator puts between us, no one has confidence in treaties: the more ceremoniously and solemnly the knot of a treaty is tied, the more quickly it is untied; it is easy to find some defect in the wording, which they often intentionally devise with some clever loophole, so that the language can never bind them so tightly that they cannot somehow escape, breaking both the treaty and their word. If such craftiness, or rather downright fraud and deceit, occurred in a private transaction it would be contemptuously decried as sacrilegious and deserving of the gallows—and that by the very same persons who are proud of having advised the prince to do the same. Thus it happens that justice seems either to be nothing more than a plebeian and humble virtue, far beneath the exalted dignity of a king, or at least there seem to be two kinds of justice: one is fit for ordinary people, lowly and creeping along the ground, fenced in on all sides, totally encumbered with chains and unable to escape; the other kind is a virtue proper to princes, which is more august than the ordinary virtue and hence much freer— forbidden, in fact, to do only what it does not wish to do.

Such behavior on the part of the princes there, who have so little respect for treaties, is the reason, I think, that the Utopians make no treaties; perhaps they would change their minds if they lived here. But even if treaties were strictly observed, they still think the practice of making them at all is a bad custom because it implies that nations think they are natural-born enemies to each other (just as if there were no natural ties between two peoples separated only by a little distance, a hill or a creek) and that they would rightly try to destroy one another if they were not bound by treaties; and that even if they have entered into a treaty, they are not united in friendship but rather have permission to prey upon each other, insofar as nothing which the treaty forbids is couched with sufficient care because of some oversight in the language. On the other hand, the Utopians think that no one should be considered an enemy if he has done no harm, and that the natural bond which unites us should replace treaties, and that men are more adequately bound to one another by good will than by agreements, more strongly joined by their hearts than by their words.

MILITARY PRACTICES

They loathe war as positively bestial (though no sort of beast engages in it as constantly as mankind), and unlike almost all nations they consider nothing more inglorious than glory won in warfare.[232] Therefore, though they regularly devote them-selves to military training on certain appointed days so that they will not be incapable of fighting when circumstances require it—and not only the men do so but also the women—they are reluctant to go to war and do so only to defend their own territory, or to drive an invading enemy from the territory of their friends, or else, out of compassion and humanity, they use their forces to liberate an oppressed people from tyranny and servitude. When they come to the aid of their friends, it is not always to defend them but sometimes also to requite and avenge injuries inflicted on them. But they do this only if they have been consulted before any steps are taken and if, after they have verified the facts, demanded restitution, and been refused, they themselves declare war.[233] They decide to do this not only when an enemy has invaded and plundered one of their friends, but also, and even more fiercely, when their friends' merchants in any part of the world have been unjustly accused under some pretext of justice, either by using unjust laws speciously or by interpreting good laws perversely.

This was the only reason for the war which the Utopians fought a little before our time on behalf of the Nephelogetes against the Alaopolitans:[234] some Nephelogete merchants among the Alaopolitans had been treated unjustly under some pretext of justice (or so the merchants thought). Certainly, whether the cause was just or unjust, it was avenged by a hideous war, in which the surrounding nations also added their energy and resources to the hostile forces of the major opponents so that some prosperous peoples were ravaged, others were badly shaken. One disaster followed upon another until finally the surrender and enslavement of the Alaopolitans put an end to the war. The Utopians, who sought nothing for themselves, subjected the vanquished to the Nephelogetes—a people hardly to be compared with the Alaopolitans in their heyday.

So fierce are the Utopians even when they are punishing only monetary injuries against their friends; but they are not so when the injury is against themselves. If they should be cheated out of their property, as long as they are subjected to no physical force, they set limits to their anger: they merely refrain from trade with that nation until restitution is made, not because they care less for their own citizens than for their allies but rather they are more offended by their friends' loss of money than by their own because their friends' merchants are severely injured by such a loss, since it comes from their own private possessions. But their own citizens lose nothing but public property, goods which were abundant at home, even superfluous, for otherwise they would not have been exported. So the loss is hardly perceived by anyone. Hence they feel that it would be cruel to punish an injury by killing many people when it causes no inconvenience to any of the Utopians in their lives or livelihood. But if any of their citizens is unjustly disabled or killed, wherever it may be, whether it be done by a public decision or by a private citizen, they send ambassadors to ascertain the facts, and if the malefactors are not handed over to them they cannot be put off but declare war immediately. If the guilty persons are handed over for punishment, they are sentenced to death or servitude.

They are not only grieved by a bloody victory but also ashamed of it, thinking that it is stupid to pay too much for merchandise, however valuable it may be. But if they conquer and crush an enemy by skill and cunning, they glory mightily in the victory, holding public parades to celebrate it and putting up a monument as if for a hard-won victory. For they boast that they have acted with courage and fortitude only when they have won the victory as no other creature but man is able to win it, that is, by the power of his wits. For bears, lions, boars, wolves, dogs, and other animals (they say) fight with the power of their bodies; and though most of them surpass us in strength and ferocity, we outdo them all in intelligence and reasoning.

Their one and only aim in warfare is to gain the objective which, if they had obtained it beforehand, would have kept them from going to war at all. Or, if circumstances make that impossible, they seek to punish those they consider culpable so severely that fear will keep them from daring to do such a thing in the future. These are the goals they set for their undertaking, and they try to achieve them quickly, but yet in such a way that a concern for avoiding danger takes precedence over winning praise and glory.

And so, immediately after declaring war, they see to it that many notices certified by their official seal are put up secretly and simultaneously in the most conspicuous places in the enemy's territory, promising a huge reward to anyone who does away with the enemy's prince; they also assign lesser, but still very substantial, sums for the deaths of those individuals they list in the same notices. These are the persons who, apart from the prince himself, were responsible for plotting against the Utopians. They double the reward assigned to the assassin if he brings them any of the proscribed persons alive; in fact, they offer the same rewards to the proscribed persons themselves, and throw immunity into the bargain, if they turn against their comrades. Thus their enemies quickly suspect all outsiders and even among themselves they are neither trusting nor trustworthy so that they live in a state of utter panic and no less peril. For it has very often turned out (as is well known) that a good number of them, and among them the prince himself, have often been betrayed by those they trusted the most. So easy is it to get someone to commit any crime whatsoever by means of bribes, and for that reason the Utopians set no limits to their bribes. Keeping in mind the great risks they are urging people to take, they take care to balance the magnitude of the danger with the lavishness of the reward; hence they promise not only enormous quantities of gold but also personal and perpetual title to rich estates in the safe and secure territory of their friends, and they faithfully keep their promises.

Other nations condemn this practice of bidding for and buying off an enemy as a barbarous, degenerate crime, but the Utopians think it does them great credit: it shows them to be wise, since in this way they win great wars without fighting at all, and also humane and compassionate, since by killing a few malefactors they spare the lives of many innocent persons who would have fallen in battle, both their own soldiers and those of the enemy; for they pity the rank-and-file of the enemy's soldiers almost as much as their own citizens because they know they do not go to war of their own accord but are driven to it by the madness of princes.

If this procedure is not successful, they sow and cultivate the seeds of dissension by encouraging the brother of the prince or some nobleman to have hopes of gaining the throne. If such internal factions languish, they stir up neighboring peoples and set them against their enemy by digging up some ancient claim such as is never lacking to kings.

When they have promised resources for war, they supply money lavishly, but their citizens very sparingly. They hold their own people so very dear and value each other so highly that they would not be willing to exchange a single one of their own citizens for the enemy's prince. But they are not at all reluctant to pay out gold and silver, since they keep it only for this purpose and would live no less comfortably if they spent all of it. Then too, apart from the wealth they have at home, they also have a limitless treasure abroad, since many nations, as I said before, owe them money. And so they hire mercenaries from everywhere and send them to war, especially the Zapoletes.[235]

These people live five hundred miles to the east of Utopia.[236] Rough, rude, and fierce, they prefer to live in the forests and rugged mountains where they were brought up. They are a hardy people, able to endure heat, cold, and hard labor. They have no interest in agriculture, no acquaintance with refinements, no concern about their houses or clothes; they care only about their flocks. They live mostly from hunting and plundering. They are born only for warfare; they zealously seek opportunities to fight and when they find one they embrace it eagerly. They set out in great numbers and offer themselves cheaply to whoever needs soldiers. The only skill they have to live on is one that aims at death.

They fight fiercely and with complete loyalty for whoever pays them. But they bind themselves for no fixed period. They sign on with the stipulation that if an enemy offers them higher wages tomorrow they will take his side, and if they are lured with slightly higher pay they will return to the side they abandoned. There are very few wars in which a great many of them are not fighting in both armies. And so it happens every day that blood relatives who were hired by the same side and lived together amicably are separated a little later in opposing armies and fight each other as enemies. Forgetting both kinship and friendship, they run each other through with violent hostility, trying to kill each other for no other reason than that they were hired for a pittance by opposing princes. They reckon their wages so strictly that adding one penny to their daily pay can easily cause them to change sides. They have quickly become greedy through and through, and yet it does them no good for what they gain with their blood they immediately squander on debauchery, and wretched debauchery at that.

These people fight for the Utopians against any mortals whatsoever because they hire their services for more than they can get anywhere else. And just as the Utopians seek good men in order to use them, so too they also enlist these wicked men in order to use them up. When they need to use them, they urge them on with great promises and expose them to the greatest dangers so that most of them do not return to claim what they were promised. To the survivors they faithfully keep their promises so as to make them eager to undertake similar exploits. Nor do they have any qualms about doing away with so many of them, since they believe the human race would owe them a great debt of gratitude if they could purge the whole world of such loathsome and wicked scum.

Apart from the Zapoletes, they use the forces of those for whom they have taken up arms, and after that the auxiliary troops of other friendly nations. As a last resort they add their own citizens, from whom they choose a man of proven valour to command the whole army. Under him they appoint two men who remain private citizens as long as he is safe, but if he is captured or killed, one of the two succeeds him, and in case of a mishap he himself is succeeded by the third, so that if the commander is in danger (and the fortunes of war are quite various) the whole army does not panic.

In each city they choose troops from a list of volunteers. No one is sent out to foreign wars against his will, for they are convinced that if someone is by nature fearful he will not only not fight vigorously himself but he will also inspire fear in his comrades. But if their country is invaded during a war, cowards of this sort, as long as they are physically fit, are dispersed among better troops in the ships or they are spread out here and there on the walls so that they have no place to run away to. Thus shame in the presence of their friends, the confrontation with the enemy, and the absence of any hope of escaping overcome fear, and often they make a virtue out of extreme necessity.

Though no one is sent to a foreign war unwillingly, if women are willing to accompany their husbands to battle the Utopians are so far from preventing them that they exhort them to do so and encourage them with praise. Each accompanies her husband to the front and is stationed shoulder to shoulder with him in the battle line. Moreover, each soldier is surrounded by his children and relatives by blood or marriage so that they all have help close by from the persons who are by nature most highly motivated to help one another. It is a great disgrace for one spouse to return without the other or for a son to come back after the loss of a parent. The result is that once it comes to hand-to-hand combat, if the enemy stands his ground, the battle is so long and grim that it ends in a general slaughter.

Certainly they take every precaution to avoid having to fight themselves, as long as they can wage war using mercenaries to take their place. But when they can no longer avoid entering the fray, the courage with which they fight matches the prudence with which they avoided fighting as long as they could. They do not give their all in a first furious attack but rather they grow stronger gradually and over a period of time, and they are so resolute that they would rather die than retreat. For one thing, they are certain that everyone at home is provided for, and they do not need to worry about their children (such concern generally breaks the spirits of lofty souls); so their courage is proud and contemptuous of defeat. Moreover, their skill in the arts of war gives them confidence. Finally, sound ideas, instilled in them from childhood on, both by instruction and through the institutions of the commonwealth, give them courage: they hold life neither so cheap as to throw it away recklessly nor so perversely dear as to cling to it greedily and shamefully when honor requires them to give it up.

When the battle is at its fiercest everywhere, a picked group of sworn and dedicated young men seek out the enemy commander.[237] Sometimes they attack him openly; sometimes they try to ambush him. They assail him from close by and from a distance and they attack him in a wide, unbroken phalanx, continuously replacing the exhausted men with fresh troops. And unless he saves himself by running away, it rarely happens that he is not killed or captured alive by his enemies.

If they win a victory, they do not slaughter the defeated; they would rather capture than kill those they have put to flight. And they never pursue retreating troops without keeping in reserve at least one battalion drawn up under its colors. They do this so regularly that if the rest of their own forces have been defeated and they win the victory with their last battalion, they would rather let the whole enemy army escape than get into the habit of pursuing the fugitives with their own forces in disarray. They remember something that happened to them more than once: when the main body of the whole Utopian army had been overwhelmed and put to flight, while the enemy was exulting in the victory and pursuing them as they ran away in all directions, a few of their own troops held in reserve and on the lookout for opportunities suddenly attacked the enemy troops, who were scattered and straggling and careless from overconfidence, and thus changed the whole outcome of the battle; snatching certain and undoubted victory from their enemies' hands, the conquered turned the tables and conquered the conquerors.

It is not easy to say whether they are more clever in laying ambushes or more cautious in avoiding them. You would think they are preparing to flee when that is the last thing they intend; on the other hand, when they do intend to flee, you would imagine that is the last thing they have in mind. For if they feel they are at a disadvantage either in numbers or location, then they either move their camp silently at night, or escape by some stratagem, or withdraw gradually by day, keeping their ranks in such good order that they are no less dangerous in retreat than when they attack. They fortify their camp very carefully with a wide and very deep moat; the earth they dig up is piled up on the inside. In such work they do not use the services of common laborers. It is done by the hands of the soldiers themselves, and the whole army joins in the work except for the armed soldiers outside the rampart who keep watch against sudden attacks. With so many soldiers pitching in, they build massive fortifications around a large area with incredible speed.

They wear armor which is strong enough to ward off blows but does not hinder movement and gestures—so much so that they feel no inconvenience even in swimming. For swimming in armor is one of the ordinary rudiments of their military training. At long range their weapon is the arrow which they shoot with great force and accuracy, not only on foot but also from horseback. At close quarters they strike not with swords but with battle-axes, which are deadly because of their sharp blade and their weight, whether used to hack or thrust. They are very skilled in devising siege engines. Once they are made, they conceal them very carefully, lest they become known before it is time to use them and turn out to be more ridiculous than useful. In designing them their primary concern is to make them easy to move and aim.

When they make a truce with their enemies, they keep it so religiously that they do not violate it even under provocation. They do not lay enemy territory waste or burn their crops; they even do what they can to keep the grain from being trampled by men and horses, for they think it may be of some use to them. They injure no unarmed civilians except for spies. They offer amnesty to cities that surrender and even those taken by siege they do not sack; instead they execute those who prevented the surrender; they enslave the rest of the defenders, but the civilian populace they leave unharmed. If they find persons who urged the town to surrender, they grant them a share in the property of the condemned; they divide up the rest and give it to their auxiliaries, for none of the Utopians takes any of the booty.

When the war is over, they assess the costs not against the friends for whom they incurred them but against the losers; they demand part of it in money, which they reserve for similar use in warfare, and part in estates within enemy territory, from which they forever enjoy a not inconsiderable income. They now have revenues of this sort in many nations; it accumulated gradually in various ways and now amounts to 700,000 ducats a year.[238] To take care of it they send out collectors of revenue, who live there in grand style and play the part of great lords. But there is plenty left over to put into the treasury,[239] unless they choose to give credit to the nation that owes it, which they often do until they need it, and even then it rarely happens that they demand all of it. They also bestow some of these estates on those whom they have persuaded to place themselves in great danger, as I mentioned before.

If some prince takes up arms against them and is preparing to invade their domain, they immediately confront him with a huge force outside their own boundaries, for they are reluctant to wage war within their own territory and no exigency could ever induce them to allow foreign auxiliaries on their island.

THE RELIGIONS OF THE UTOPIANS
There are various religions not only throughout the island but also within individual cities: some worship the sun as god,

others the moon, others a different planet. Others worship some ancient paragon of either virtue or glory, venerating such a person not only as a god but as the supreme god. But the vast majority, and those by far the wiser ones, accept none of those gods and believe there is a certain single deity, unknown, eternal, infinite, inexplicable, diffused throughout this whole universe not physically but by his power, in a manner that is beyond human comprehension; him they call their parent. To him alone they attribute the origin, increase, progress, changes, and goals of all things; him and no other they honor as divine.

Actually, though all the others hold different beliefs on some points, they agree with the monotheists in thinking that there is some one supreme being who made and rules the universe, and in their native language they all agree in calling him Mythras,[240] but they differ in that they identify the supreme power variously, each asserting that whatever he considers to be supreme is in fact that single nature to whose divine majesty, by the consensus of all nations, the whole creation is attributed. But gradually they are all abandoning these superstitious variations and joining together in that one religion which seems more reasonable than the others. And there is no doubt that the other beliefs would have vanished long ago if it were not that, whenever something untoward happened to someone who was considering changing his religion, fear made him think that it was not accidental but was sent from heaven, as if the divinity whose cult he was forsaking were avenging a wicked affront to himself.

But after they had heard from us the name, the teaching, the behavior, and the miracles of Christ, and the no less miraculous constancy of so many martyrs who freely shed their blood and thus brought many peoples, from far and wide, over to their religion, you would not believe how eagerly they also were converted, whether through the secret inspiration of God or because Christianity seemed closest to the sect which is predominant among them, although I think it was a matter of no small moment with them to hear that Christ approved of life in common for his disciples and that it is still practiced among the most genuine Christian communities.[241] But certainly, whatever the reason, no small number of them were converted to our religion and were washed clean in the sacred waters of baptism.

But because there was, I am sorry to say, no priest among the four of us (for only that number remained after two of us had given up the ghost), they received the other sacraments but still lacked those which among us are conferred only by priests.[242] But they know about them and long for them most intensely. In fact, they also earnestly discuss among themselves whether someone chosen from among their number could receive the sacerdotal character[243] without the dispatch of a Christian bishop. And in fact it seemed they were about to choose someone, but when I left they had not yet done so.

Even those who do not agree with the Christian religion still do not frighten anyone away from it; they do not oppose anyone who has embraced it, except that one of our community was repressed while I was there. Shortly after he was baptized, over our objections, he harangued publicly about Christianity with more zeal than prudence, and he began to get so carried away that he not only ranked our religion above all the rest but condemned all the others outright. He cried out against them as profane; he denounced their worshipers as wicked, sacrilegious, and worthy to be punished in eternal fire.

When he had preached like this for a long time, they arrested him and tried him, not for despising their religion but for exciting riots among the people.[244] They convicted him and sentenced him to exile, for it is one of their oldest policies that no one should come to any harm because of his religion.

For Utopus had learned that before his arrival the inhabitants squabbled incessantly about religion and he had noticed that the sects, which generally disagreed with each other and fought for their country in separate groups, provided the opportunity for him to conquer all of them. Hence, from the very beginning, after he had obtained the victory, he decreed first of all that everyone could practice the religion of his choice and could also strive to convert others to it, but only so long as he advocated it calmly and moderately with rational arguments. And if he could not win others over by persuasion, he was not to assail their religions bitterly nor use force against them, and he was to refrain from insults. Anyone who quarrels insolently about religion is punished with exile or enslavement.[245]

Utopus laid down these rules not only for the sake of peace, which he saw was completely undermined by constant strife and implacable hatred, but also because he thought such a decree would benefit religion itself. In religious matters he did not venture to dogmatize rashly because he was uncertain whether or not God wishes to have varied and manifold kinds of worship and hence inspires different people with different views. Certainly he thought that to use force and threats to make everyone accept what you believe to be true is both arrogant and absurd. Then too, if one religion should be actually true and the rest false, still he easily foresaw that in the long run the the truth would sooner or later emerge and prevail by its own force as long as the matter was handled reasonably and moderately. But if the struggle is conducted with arms and uprisings, since the worst people are always the most headstrong, the best and holiest religion, embroiled among empty superstitions, will be choked like grain among thorns and briars. And so he left the whole matter open and left everyone free to believe whatever he wanted, except that he solemnly and strictly forbade that anyone should sink so far below the dignity of human nature as to think that the soul dies with the body or that the world is ruled by mere chance and not by providence.

And for this reason they believe that after this life punishments are ordained for vices and rewards for virtues. Anyone who thinks otherwise they do not even include in the category of human beings since he has degraded the lofty nature of his soul to the base level of a beast's wretched body. Still less will they count him as one of their citizens, since he would set no store whatever by all their laws and morality if it were not for fear. For who can doubt that someone who has nothing to fear but the law and no hope of anything beyond bodily existence would strive to evade the public laws of his country by secret chicanery or to break them by force in order to satisfy his own personal greed? For that reason they bestow no honors on such a person, they assign him to no office, they put him in charge of no public responsibility. He is universally looked down on as a lazy and spineless character. But he is not subjected to any punishment because they are convinced that it is not within a person's power to believe whatever he wishes; they neither compel him by any threats to mask his opinion nor accept any pretexts or lies, which they utterly despise as next door to deliberate malice. Still they do forbid him to argue for his opinion, but only among the common people. Otherwise, in private, among priests and prudent men, they not only permit him to argue but also encourage it, confident that in the end his madness will yield to reason.

There are also others, and they are by no means few (since their position is not forbidden as completely unreasonable or wicked) who go to the opposite extreme and believe that the souls of brute beasts are also immortal, although not comparable to ours in dignity nor destined for the same happiness.[246]

Almost all of them are certain and fully persuaded that human happiness will be so boundless that they mourn for everyone who is sick but not for anyone who dies, unless they see that he is torn from life anxiously and unwillingly. For they take this to be a very bad sign, as if such a soul, despairing and conscious of guilt, fears to leave life because of some secret presentiment of future punishment. Moreover, they think God will hardly be well pleased when someone who is summoned does not come running eagerly but is dragged off reluctant and unwilling. Therefore when they see such a death they are dismayed and they carry out the dead persons with grief and in silence; after praying that God in his mercy will kindly forgive the infirmities of such souls, they cover the body with earth. On the other hand, when someone dies joyfully and full of good hope, they do not mourn him, but rather they conduct his funeral with song; commending his soul to God with great affection, they finally cremate his body with reverence, not grief, and erect on that spot a column inscribed with the virtues of the dead person. After they have returned home, they tell of his character and deeds, and no part of his life is rehearsed more often or more eagerly than his cheerful death.

They think this commemoration of his uprightness is a very strong inducement to virtue for the living and the most acceptable form of veneration to the dead, whom they also believe to be present when they are talked about, though invisible to us because the eyesight of mortals is too dull to see them. For it would not be suitable to the condition of the blessed to lack the liberty of going wherever they want, and it would be ungrateful of them to have no desire whatever to visit their friends, to whom they were united in mutual love and charity while they were alive; such charity they suppose, like other good qualities, is increased, not diminished, in good men after their death.[247] Thus they believe that the dead are present among the living, observing what they say and do, and for that reason they go about their business more confidently because of their trust in such protectors; their belief in the presence of their ancestors also deters them from secret wrongdoing.

They have nothing to do with fortune-telling and other vain, superstitious divinations, which other people take quite seriously but which they consider ridiculous. But miracles which happen apart from any natural cause they revere as works and witnesses which manifest the presence of a deity. They say such miracles often happen there, and sometimes, during great crises, they pray publicly for a miracle with great confidence and they do obtain it.

They think the worship which pleases God is the contemplation of nature and the praise which springs from it. But there are others, and they are by no means few, who neglect learning in the name of religion, who do not strive to attain any knowledge, and who allow themselves no leisure at all.[248] They are determined to earn happiness after death solely by keeping busy in the service of others. And so some tend the sick, others repair the roads, clear out ditches, rebuild bridges, dig turf, sand, or stones, fell and cut up trees, cart lumber, crops, and other provisions into the cities. They perform their services not only for the public but also for private citizens, and they work even harder than slaves. They willingly and cheerfully undertake any tasks which are rough, difficult, dirty, and shunned by most people because of the toil, disgust, and hopelessness they entail. They see to it that others have leisure, while they themselves are continually engaged in labor and toil, but nevertheless they take no credit for it. They neither censure the lives of others nor extol their own. The more they conduct themselves like slaves the more everyone honors them.

They are divided into two sects. The one is celibate and not only abstains from any sexual activity but also eats no meat (and some of them no animal products at all), totally rejecting the pleasures of this life as harmful, longing only for those of the world to come, which they strive to obtain by toil and vigils. Meanwhile, confident that they will soon obtain them, they are cheerful and energetic. The other group, no less devoted to labor, prefers to marry: they do not spurn the consolations of marriage, and they think that just as they owe such activity to nature, they owe children to their country. They do not refuse any pleasure which does not interfere with their work. They like to eat the flesh of animals precisely because they think such food gives them the strength to do all kinds of work. The Utopians consider this group more prudent; the other they regard as holier. If they claimed on rational grounds to prefer celibacy to marriage and a hard life to a comfortable one, the Utopians would laugh at them; but since they profess to be motivated by religion, the Utopians respect and revere them. On no other subject are they more cautious about making any rash pronouncements than on matters concerning religion. In their language these persons are given the special title "Buthrescae," which could be translated into Latin as "religiosi."[249]

Their priests are extremely holy and therefore very few. For each city has no more than thirteen, one for each church, except during wartime, when seven of them set out with the army and are replaced by substitutes for the time being. But when the priests return, each assumes his former position. Until the time when the substitutes, in an orderly succession, replace priests who have died, they become attendants of the high priest (for one priest has authority over the others). They are elected by the people in the same way as other magistrates, that is, by secret ballot, in order to avoid partisan strife. Once elected, they are consecrated by their own college of priests.

They preside over divine worship, attend to religious matters, and act as guardians of morality. To be summoned by them and rebuked for dishonorable conduct is considered to be a great disgrace. But their role is to exhort and admonish; to repress and punish wrongdoers is the function of the ruler and other magistrates. The priests, however, do excommunicate those they find to be thoroughly vicious. There is almost no other punishment which they fear more, for such persons are both dejected by their infamy and tormented by a bad conscience. They may not even be physically safe for very long. For unless they quickly convince the priests that they are repentant, they will be seized by the senate and punished for their impiety.

Children and young people are educated by the priests, and they devote no more attention to learning than to character and virtue.[250] They take the greatest pains from the very first to instill in the tender and impressionable minds of children sound opinions conducive to preserving the common good. When such ideas are thoroughly absorbed in childhood, they persist throughout all of manhood and they are extremely useful in protecting the status of the commonwealth, which decays only because of vices which spring from perverse attitudes.

The wives of the priests are the very finest women in the country, unless the priests themselves are women, for that sex is not excluded; but they are rarely elected and must be widows of advanced years.[251]

No magistrates are held in greater honor among the Utopians, so much so that even if they commit a crime they are not subject to a public tribunal but are left to God and their own consciences. For they do not think it is right to lay human hands on anyone, however vicious, who has been dedicated to God in such a special way as a holy offering, so to speak. It is easier for them to observe this custom because priests are so few and are chosen so carefully. For it is very unlikely that someone who is the cream of the crop and is elevated to a position of such dignity only because of his virtue should degenerate into corruption and vice. And even if that very thing should happen—for human nature is changeable—nevertheless there would certainly be no reason to fear that the public would be in any great danger, because the priests are so few and have no power beyond what derives from the honor paid them. In fact the very reason they have so few and scattered priests is to keep the dignity of the order, now held in such high esteem, from being cheapened by bestowing the honor on many, especially since they think it is hard to find very many who are equal to the dignity of the office, for which merely mediocre virtues are insufficient.[252]

Their reputation at home is no greater than the esteem in

which they are held by foreign nations. This becomes quite clear, I think, if we note the reason for it. When troops are engaged in battle, the priests kneel at a distance but not very far away, dressed in their sacred vestments; lifting up their hands to heaven, they pray first of all for peace, and then for victory for their own forces, but without bloodshed on either side.[253] When their soldiers win they rush into the battle line and restrain the fury of their forces against the routed troops. Merely to see them and make oneself known to them by calling out is enough to save anyone's life; to touch their flowing garments also protects the remaining goods of fortune from any damage due to the war. Hence they are venerated by the countries all around them, who attribute to them such genuine majesty that oftentimes they provide as much protection for their own citizens as they do for their enemies. For sometimes it has happened that, when their battle line was thrown back in despair and had turned to flee, as the enemy was rushing in to kill and plunder, the intervention of the priests has stopped the slaughter and separated the two armies so that a peace was devised and established on equitable terms. For nowhere is there a nation so savage, cruel, and barbarous that they do not hold their persons to be sacrosanct and inviolable.

The first and last days of each month and likewise of each year are celebrated as feastdays; the months are marked off by the orbit of the moon, just as the year is established by the course of the sun. In their language they call all of the first days "cynemerni," the last days "trapemerni,"[254] names that are equivalent to "first-feastday" and "last-feastday." Their churches are remarkable not only for their workmanship but also for their capacity to hold immense crowds—which is necessary because there are so few of them.[255] They are all dimly lit, and they say this resulted not from lack of skill but from the deliberate policy of the priests, who believe that too much light distracts our thoughts, whereas dim and doubtful lighting concentrates the mind and intensifies religious devotion.

Since religion is not the same for everyone there, yet all the forms of it, however varied and different, converge from various directions on one goal, the worship of the divine nature, nothing is seen or heard in the churches which is not held in common by all the religions. If any denomination has a rite peculiar to it, they provide for it in their own homes. Public worship is conducted according to a ritual which does not at all detract from any of the private devotions. Therefore no images of the gods are seen in churches so that everyone can be free to imagine the form of God as he wishes according to his own religion. They invoke God by no other name than Mythras, a name they all apply to the one divine nature, whatever it may be. No prayers are devised which everyone cannot say without offending his own denomination.

And so on the last-feastdays they gather in church in the evening, still fasting and ready to give thanks to God for the success they enjoyed during the year or month just coming to an end. On the next day, which is the first-feastday, they flock to church in the morning to pray for success and happiness in the following year or month which begins on that feastday. But on the last-feastdays, at home, before they go to church, wives throw themselves at the feet of their husbands, and children do the same before their parents; they confess that they have sinned either through commission or negligence, and they beg forgiveness for their offenses. In this way if some little cloud of strife has arisen in the household, it is dispelled by such atonement so that they can attend the sacrifices with clear and untroubled minds, for they are too conscientious to worship with a disturbed conscience.[256] Therefore those who feel anger or hatred toward someone do not intrude on the sacrifices unless they are reconciled and purged of such feelings, for fear of some swift and severe punishment.[257]

When they get there, the men sit on the right side of the church, the women separately on the left. Then too, they position themselves so that the male members of each household sit in front of the master of that household, and the matron of each household sits in the last row of the women. Thus they see to it that all the actions of everyone are observed in public by the persons whose authority maintains discipline at home. Moreover they are also very careful to intermingle everywhere young persons with their elders; otherwise, if children were entrusted to children, they might spend in childish tomfoolery the time that they should devote to cultivating a religious fear of the heavenly beings,[258] the greatest and practically the only incitement to virtue.[259]

In their sacrifices they do not kill any animals; they do not think that a merciful God, who bestowed life on animals precisely that they might live, takes any pleasure in bloodshed and slaughter. They burn incense and other fragrant substances. They also display many candles, not because they do not know that such things add nothing to God's nature, no more than human prayers do, but they like this harmless mode of worship and people feel that somehow such perfumes, lights, and other ceremonies lift up the human heart and make it rise more eagerly in divine worship.

In church the people wear white garments; the priests are

127

clothed in vestments of various colors, marvelous in both workmanship and design, though the materials are not especially expensive, and they are not woven with gold threads or encrusted with rare gems; rather they are fashioned out of the feathers of various birds, so elegantly and skillfully that the costliest material would not match the value of the workmanship.[260] Moreover, these feathers and plumes of birds and the set patterns in which they are arranged on the priests' garments are said to contain certain secret mysteries which, if rightly understood (and the interpretation is carefully handed down by the priests), remind them of the benefits bestowed on them by God and of the devotion they owe him in return, as well as their duty to each other.

When the priest, dressed in this way, comes out of the sacristy, everyone immediately prostrates himself on the ground out of reverence; on all sides the silence is so profound that the spectacle itself inspires a certain fear, as if in the presence of some divinity. They remain on the ground for a while and then arise at a signal from the priest. Then they sing the praises of God, accompanied by musical instruments, which are mostly shaped differently from those seen in our part of the world. Most of them surpass ours in sweetness of tone, but some of them are incomparably superior to ours. But in one respect their music is undoubtedly far ahead of ours: whether instrumental or vocal, it imitates and expresses natural feelings so well, the sound matches the sense of the words so closely (whether they express supplication or joy, peace or turmoil, sadness or anger), and the shape of the melody matches the meaning so well that it quite wonderfully stirs up, pierces, and inflames the hearts of the hearers.[261] Finally the priest and the people recite together certain customary and fixed forms of prayer, composed in such a way that everyone can apply to himself what they all recite together.

In these prayers each one recognizes God as the creator and ruler of the universe and also the source of all good things. He thanks God for bestowing so many benefits on him, but especially because through God's kindness he was placed in the happiest form of commonwealth and has been allotted the religion which he hopes is the truest. If he is mistaken in this matter or if there is some form of commonwealth or religion which is better and more approved by God, he prays that God in his goodness will cause him to recognize it, for he is prepared to follow wherever God leads him. But if this form of commonwealth is the best and this religion is truest, he asks that God will both make him steadfast and lead other mortals to the same way of life and the same idea of God—unless there is in fact something in this variety of religions which pleases his inscrutable will.

Finally he prays that by an easy death God may take him to himself, how soon or late he certainly does not dare to determine. But, provided that God's majesty is not offended by it, he would much rather go to him by a very difficult death than be kept away from him any longer, even by a prosperous way of life. After saying this prayer they once more prostrate themselves on the ground and after a little while they get up again, go to eat lunch, and spend the rest of the day playing games or doing military exercises.

I have described to you as accurately as I can the plan of their commonwealth, which I certainly consider to be not only the best but also the only kind worthy of the name. For elsewhere they always talk about the public good but they are concerned with their own private welfare; here,[262] where there is no private property, everyone works seriously for the public good. And for good reason in both places, for elsewhere is there anyone who does not know that unless he looks out for his own personal interest he will die of hunger, no matter how flourishing the commonwealth may be; therefore necessity causes him to think he should watch out for his own good, not that of others, that is, of the people. On the other hand, here, where everything belongs to everyone, no one doubts that (as long as care is taken that the public storehouses are full) nothing whatever will be lacking to anyone for his own use. For the distribution of goods is not niggardly; no one is a pauper or a beggar there, and though no one has anything, all are rich.

For what greater wealth can there be than to be completely spared any anxiety and to live with a joyful and tranquil frame of mind, with no worries about making a living, not vexed by a wife's complaints and demands, not fearing a son will end up in poverty, not concerned about a daughter's dowry, but secure about the livelihood and happiness of himself and his own, his wife, children, grandchildren, great-grandchildren, great-great-grandchildren, and however long a line of descendants noblemen presume they will have. Indeed those who worked before but are now disabled are no less provided for than those who are still working.

At this point I wish that someone would venture to compare with this equity the justice to be found in other nations, where I'll be damned if I can find any trace whatever of justice or equity. For what sort of justice is it for some nobleman or goldsmith[263] or moneylender or, in short, any of the others who either do nothing at all or something that is not very necessary for the commonwealth, to live luxuriously and splendidly in complete idleness or doing some superfluous task?

And at the same time a laborer, a teamster, a blacksmith or farmer works so long and so hard that a beast of burden could hardly sustain it, performing tasks so necessary that without them no commonwealth could survive at all for even a single year, and yet they earn such a meager living and lead such miserable lives that beasts of burden seem to be better off, since they do not have to work so incessantly, their fodder is not much worse (and to them it tastes better), and in the meantime they are not afraid of what will happen to them. These workers are driven to toil without profit or gain in the present; they are crushed by the thought that they will be poverty-stricken in their old age, for their daily wages are not enough for that very day, much less can they accumulate any surplus which might be put aside every day to provide for their old age.

Is a commonwealth not unjust and ungrateful if it lavishes so many benefits on noblemen, as they are called, and goldsmiths, and the rest of that crew who are either idle or else merely flatterers and providers of empty pleasures, but makes no proper provision for farmers, colliers, laborers, teamsters, and blacksmiths, without whom there would be no commonwealth at all; unmindful of their sleepless labors and forgetting their many and great contributions, it first uses up the labors of their flourishing years, and then, when they are worn down by old age and diseases, it is totally ungrateful and rewards them with a miserable death. And how about this: every day the rich scrape away something from the wages of the poor, not only by private chicanery but also by public laws. Before, it seemed unjust that those who deserve the most from the commonwealth should receive the least, but now, by promulgating a law, they have transmuted this perversion into justice. From my observation and experience of all the flourishing nations everywhere, what is taking place, so help me God, is nothing but a conspiracy of the rich, as it were, who look out for themselves under the pretext of serving the commonwealth.[264] They think up and devise all ways and means, first of keeping (and having no fear of losing) what they have heaped up through underhanded deals, and then of taking advantage of the poor by buying their labor and toil as cheaply as possible. Once the rich have decreed in the name of the public (including the poor) that these schemes must be observed, then they become laws.

But after these depraved creatures, in their insatiable greed, have divided among themselves all the goods which would have sufficed for everyone, they are still very far from the happiness of the Utopian commonwealth; there, once the use of money was abolished, and together with it all greed for it, what a mass of troubles was cut away, what a crop of crimes was pulled up by the roots! Is there anyone who does not know that fraud, theft, plunder, strife, turmoil, contention, rebellion, murder, treason, poisoning, crimes which are constantly punished but never held in check, would die away if money were eliminated? And also that at the very instant when money disappeared, so would fear, anxiety, worries, toil, and sleepless nights? Indeed, poverty itself, which seems to be merely the lack of money, would itself immediately fade away if money were everywhere totally abolished.

To make this clearer, imagine some barren year of bad harvests when many thousands of people die of hunger. I maintain it is clear that at the end of this famine, if you examined the barns of the rich, you would find so much grain that if it had been divided among those swept away by starvation and disease, no one would have noticed any effect at all of the failure of weather and soil. It would have been easy to provide food if that blessed money, that invention very clearly designed to open the way to what we need to live, were not the only barrier to keep us from it. I have no doubt that the rich also understand this and are not unaware how much better it would be to lack no necessities than to abound in so many superfluities, to be relieved of so many troubles than to be hemmed in by such great wealth. And in fact I have no doubt that everyone's concern for his own well-being or the authority of our savior Christ (who is so wise that he cannot be unaware of what is best and so good that he would never advise what he knew was not the best) would long since have easily drawn the whole world to adopt the laws of this commonwealth, if it were not held back by one and only one monster, the prince and parent of all plagues, pride.[265]

Pride measures prosperity not by her own advantages but by the disadvantages of others. She would not even wish to be a goddess unless there were some wretches left whom she could order about and lord it over, whose misery would make her happiness seem all the more extraordinary, whose poverty can be tormented and exacerbated by a display of her wealth. This infernal serpent, pervading the human heart, keeps men from reforming their lives, holding them back like a suckfish.[266]

Since pride is too firmly fixed in the minds of men to be easily plucked out, I am glad that this form of commonwealth, which I would gladly see adopted by everyone, is at least enjoyed by the Utopians; they have followed ethical principles which enabled them to lay the foundations of a commonwealth that is not only most happy but also, so far as human prescience can foresee, likely to last forever. For now that they

133

have eradicated factional strife and ambition at home, along with the other vices, there is no danger that they can be disturbed by domestic discord, which has been the sole reason for the downfall of many prosperous and splendidly fortified cities. But as long as their domestic tranquility and wholesome social structure is preserved, the envy of all the surrounding princes cannot shock or unsettle their dominion, though in the past they have often unsuccessfully tried to do so.

When Raphael had ended his tale, there occurred to me quite a few institutions established by the customs and laws of that nation which seemed to me quite absurd, not only in their way of waging war, their religious beliefs and practices, and other institutions as well, but also (and above all) in the very point which is the principal foundation of their whole social structure, namely their common life and subsistence with no exchange of money. That one fact entirely undermines all nobility, magnificence, splendor, and majesty, which are (in the popular view) the true adornments and ornaments of a commonwealth.[267] Nevertheless, I knew that his talk had worn him out, and I was not sure whether he could endure to listen to an opinion contrary to his own—especially since I remembered that he had reproached some persons precisely because they thought they would not be considered wise unless they could find some way of picking apart the ideas of others—and so, having praised their regimen and his own exposition, I took his hand and led him in to dinner, though first I said we would have another time to consider these matters more thoroughly and to confer more fully. I only wish this would happen someday!

Meanwhile, just as I can hardly agree with all the points he made (even though he is a person of unquestionable learning and wide experience of human affairs), so too I readily confess that in the Utopian commonwealth are very many features which in our societies I would wish rather than expect to see.

THE END OF THE SECOND BOOK

The End of the Afternoon Discourse
of Raphael Hythloday
about the Laws and Institutions
of the Little-known Island of Utopia
Recorded by the Most Illustrious
and Learned Gentleman
Master Thomas More
Citizen and Undersheriff of London

Thomas More to His Friend Peter Giles,
Warmest Greetings

My dear Peter, I was thoroughly delighted with the judgment you know about, delivered by that very sharp fellow in the form of a dilemma directed against my *Utopia:* if the story is being presented as true, I find some things in it rather absurd; if it is a fiction, then I think that More's usual good judgment is lacking on some points. I am very grateful to this man, my dear Peter, whoever he may be, who I suspect is learned and whom I see as a friendly critic. I do not know whether any other critique since the book came out has pleased me as much as this one. For, first of all, motivated either by his regard for me or for the work itself, it seems that he did not begrudge the effort of reading it all the way through, and that not cursorily and hastily the way priests read the divine office (if they do so at all) but deliberately and carefully so as to weigh the details thoughtfully. And then, after criticizing some points, and not very many at that, he declares that he approves of the rest, not thoughtlessly but judiciously. Finally, even in the language with which he castigates me he praises me more highly than those who deliberately set out to praise me. For he gives a clear indication what a splendid opinion he has of me when he complains that he is disappointed when he reads a passage that is not as precise as it should be, whereas I myself exceed my own hopes if I happen to be able to publish something in the whole lot that is at least not absolutely absurd.

But in fact, to deal with him no less frankly in turn, I do not see why he should consider himself so eagle-eyed and, as the Greeks say, sharp-sighted, if he discovers some things rather absurd in the institutions of the Utopians or finds that in setting up a commonwealth I have not thought through some matters in a sufficiently practical way, as if there were no absurdities elsewhere in the world, or as if any of all the philosophers everywhere had so devised a commonwealth, a ruler, or a household so perfectly as to propound nothing that could not be improved. On that point, if it were not that I consider as sacred the memory of the most extraordinary men who have been hallowed from ancient times, I could certainly point out features from each of them which everyone would undoubtedly agree in condemning.

But when he is in doubt whether the work is true or fictitious, on this point I think his own usual good judgment is lacking. Nevertheless, I do not deny that if I had decided to write about the commonwealth and a story such as this had occurred to me, I would not have shrunk from a fictional presentation which would make the truth slip more pleasantly into the mind like medicine smeared with honey. But certainly I would have managed it so that, even though I might have wanted to deceive the ignorant mob, I would at least have inserted some pointed hints which would have let the more learned discover what I was about. Thus even if I had done nothing more than assign to the ruler, river, city, and island such names as would have informed learned readers that the island is nowhere, the city is a phantom, the river has no water, the ruler no people—which would not have been hard to do and would have been much more elegant than what I actually did, for if I had not been forced by historical accuracy, I am not so stupid as to use those barbarous and meaningless names Utopia, Anyder, Amaurot, and Ademus.[268]

But my dear Giles, since I see that some people are so cautious, wary, and sagacious that they can hardly be induced to believe what we simple and credulous souls wrote down at Hythloday's dictation, lest such persons should mistrust not only the accuracy of the story but also my own credibility, I am glad that I can say for my brainchild what Mysis in Terence says to keep Glycerius' boy from being considered a change-ling: "By heaven, I thank goodness that there were some free-born matrons present at the birth."[269] For luckily for me it so happens that Raphael told his tale not only to you and me but also to many very respectable and upstanding men. I do not know whether he related more numerous or notable details but I am sure he told them no fewer and no less remarkable matters than he did to us.

But if these incredulous persons will not take even their word for it, they can visit Hythloday himself, for he has not yet died. I just heard from some persons who recently re-turned from Portugal that on the first day of last March he was healthy and vigorous as ever. Therefore let them ask him for the truth or question him to ferret it out, as long as they understand that I am responsible only for my own work, not for the trustworthiness of others. Farewell, dearest Peter, to you and your charming wife and pretty little daughter, to whom my wife wishes long life and good health.

JERRY HARP

Poet, translator, lawyer, statesman, social philosopher, martyr, and (as of 1935) canonized saint, Thomas More remains—in his friend Erasmus's phrase—a "man for all seasons," one who in his integrity is suited to all occasions.[1] He was formed to no small degree by the cultural movement known as Renaissance humanism, with its emphases on the study of ancient texts, the deepening of a historical sense, the cultivation of the art of rhetoric, and devotion to active service in the world. The terms "Renaissance" and "humanism" come trailing clouds of ambiguity, so some sorting of their meaning is in order.

The idea that the Renaissance—roughly 1400 to 1650, give or take (depending on where one stood in the world)—was a time of great cultural renewal immediately following the "Dark Ages" owes a lot to the work of Jacob Burkhardt.[2] Although his writing has been immensely influential, many generations of scholars have challenged certain of his ideas.[3] More recent work has stressed, for example, the continuities that carry from the ancient, through the medieval, and into the early modern world.[4] One sign of the continuity is the occurrence of various smaller-scale renaissances leading up to the major period known as *the* Renaissance. There was the Carolingian Renaissance of the late eighth and ninth centuries, which brought into greater prominence study of the Bible, the church fathers, and the Latin classics, along with a reform of handwriting that made the copying of manuscripts more efficient. Later came the Ottonian Renaissance (tenth century), with its emphasis on historical writing, revitalization of monastic and cathedral schools, and increased circulation of classical learning. Perhaps most widely known is the Renaissance of the "long twelfth century" (roughly 1050 to 1250), which saw a surge of cultural energies in a variety of spheres: further revival of the classics of ancient Latinity, the rise of scholasticism, and the emergence of theology as an academic discipline, as well as developments in art, architecture, vernacular literature, and music.[5] These "Dark Ages" were not so dark as some reports might lead us to believe.

That there was greater continuity between the fall of Rome and the beginning of the Renaissance is one reason for the use, in the past few decades, of the term "early modern" in preference to "Renaissance." To put the matter simply, "early modern" stresses the period's relationship to what follows (modernity and even postmodernity), whereas "Renaissance" emphasizes the period's relationship to the past, and also implies that culture somehow died out in the intervening period (returning us again to the idea of the Dark Ages). While the term "early modern" avoids the problem of connoting a rebirth of something that never really died out, it also introduces its own distinct difficulties into the discussion. For example, it tends to gloss over important differences between early and late modernity, implying a smoother trajectory of cultural development than is fitting. Nevertheless, it can be salutary to choose a new set of problems to negotiate; the new questions can call forth insights and work that otherwise might not occur. Besides, in placing greater emphasis on the Renaissance as harbinger of the new, the term "early modern" actually extends the work of Burkhardt, who ends his great study by proclaiming the Italian Renaissance the "leader of modern ages."[6]

The evidence of continuity does not, however, negate that something distinctive and new was happening in the period commonly referred to as the Renaissance, merely that the Burkhardtian view of disjunction overstates the case. Taking shape in the run-up to the Renaissance is what might be termed the requisite intellectual infrastructure in the form, for example, of the many manuscripts that medieval monks had been busy copying for centuries, and then in the form of printed books in the middle of the fifteenth century. As Jack Goody has pointed out, the Renaissance of early modern Europe is one instance of an identifiable pattern in which a critical mass of material culture enables a recovery and circulation of much older texts, which in some cases then lead to an outpouring of further work and experimentation.[7] Even if many of the ancient texts had continued to be known, at least by a learned cohort, their further circulation was required to open the floodgates of Renaissance work.

A distinctive movement within the early modern era was what scholars in the nineteenth century termed humanism. Douglas Bush said of this movement that it is a "medieval fusion of classical wisdom with Christian faith, and the only real change in later times was that the classical element, philosophically and aesthetically, became a less inferior partner."[8] With regard to the aesthetic inheritance, the humanists' work brought the importance of style in human discourse into greater prominence, not as mere ornamentation but as part and parcel of signification. In other words, they emphasized rhetoric over dialectic (logic); it's not that they were against logic, but rather that they were deeply aware that far more than logic is needed to make discourse meaningful. When Aristotle defined rhetoric as the "faculty of observing in any given case the available means of persuasion," he was writing about oratory, but rhetoric also has to do with the art of structuring discourse.[9] In other words, rhetoric is about the ways that human experience, insight, and wisdom are encoded in language.

This concern with the style and structuring of discourse was at the heart of the humanists' educational and cultural reform of the medieval dispensation they inherited, and *Utopia* exemplifies these ambitions with great force.[10] In the Dialogue of Counsel,[11] when Hythloday maintains that princes would be impervious to his advice, the character More takes him to task for his idea that the language of truth is singular; Hythloday's preference is for the language of "academic philosophy" (p. 43), the scholasticism that the humanists criticized for its obsessive concern with hyper-subtle logic. As in his letter to Martin Dorp, More derided a trifling, pointless, and at times captious concern with logical quibbles.[12] Generally, the humanists wanted more Cicero and less of the Aristotle of the logical works in their educational program.

With their focus on rhetoric and style, the humanists developed the discipline of textual criticism, seeking as they did to establish reliable texts and accurate translations. A signal example of this work with texts, one that connects with the humanists' historical-mindedness, is Lorenzo Valla's demonstration that the Donation of Constantine was a forgery. Relying largely on historical details, many of them philological, Valla showed that the document could not have come from the Emperor Constantine's hand.[13]

In relation to their other labors, the humanists also undertook a variety of literary experiments, such as the classic and quirky texts by Erasmus (*Praise of Folly*), More (*Utopia*), and François Rabelais (*Gargantua and Pantagruel*). It was as if all of the scholarly work and public service issued in outbreaks of sheer creativity and serious play. For all of the lasting value of the humanists' scholarship, it is these texts at play that most of us now read most assiduously. It is not without reason that, with regard to More's text, one of the great theologians of our day discerns a strong link between utopia and festivity.[14]

The humanist emphasis on rhetoric and style fostered skills fitting for administrative workers in a world of increasingly centralized states and expanding bureaucratic church structures. These skills were fostered by such precursors of the humanists as the lawyers and notaries who mediated commercial activity in thirteenth-century Italy, workers who embellished documents and letters with allusions to the Latin classics. Further, their training in Roman law led them to study the literature of ancient Rome as well.[15] As this world of centralized bureaucracy grew, so did the need for well-trained and fluent language workers. Whatever its other merits, humanism trained people to work in this increasingly bureaucratized world, the one for which Thomas More was shaped.

His early formation took place in the grammar school (where young boys were drilled in the niceties of Latin grammar) at St. Anthony's in London. Having finished his course of study there, he embarked on an apprenticeship at the home of Archbishop (later Cardinal and then Lord Chancellor)

Morton, who shows up as a character in *Utopia*. As a page in Morton's household at Lambeth, More would have not only learned how to play a formal role on public occasions, but also extended his rhetorical skills by engaging in debates and taking on various personae to perform fluent and convincing discourses.[16] Having entered his fourteenth year, he left Lambeth to enter Canterbury College, Oxford, where he studied for two years before leaving to take up legal studies at New Inn, London. We do not know why he left Oxford without taking a degree, though it is worth noting that it was not uncommon to study at a university for a year or two before moving on to legal training. After two years at New Inn, he moved on to Lincoln's Inn to continue his training in the law. It was during his time at Lincoln's Inn that he was also part of a circle of scholars—such as William Grocyn, John Colet, and Thomas Linacre—interested in the new humanist learning. These figures came from a variety of walks of life including medicine, law, theater, education, and publishing.[17] But the most influential person More met at this time was Erasmus, who first visited England in 1499. Because neither was proficient in the other's native tongue, they spoke Latin, the lingua franca of European intellectual life, a language in which they could exchange ideas, interests, and witticisms. Early in their friendship, they undertook a friendly contest of translating work of the ancient Greek satirist Lucian from Greek into Latin. Erasmus saw *Utopia* through the press of Thierry Martens at Louvain. It appeared near the end of 1516.[18]

Utopia keeps appearing as if out of nowhere, showing up in the here and now to take us elsewhere. According to Thomas More's Greek pun, "Utopia" is the good place (*eu-topos*) that is no place (*ou-topos*). Early on he referred to his book by the

Latin *Nusquama* (Nowhere),[19] but it was his Greek coinage that entered the language, and it shows up everywhere. Although the term has come to mean an imaginary and ideal place, an impractical social scheme, More's text works in more complex ways than popular usage allows. *Utopia* is a nowhere that opens into new discursive spaces. Were the realm of the present and pragmatic concern to dominate entirely, we would be led into stagnation. The nowhere of *Utopia*—the work as well as the genre and mode of thinking—provides one way to keep consciousness on the move even though it is an impossible place (even the mathematical dimensions of the island cannot work out).[20]

More's great text indeed uncannily recurs. Many editions have been noted.[21] Back in the early 1980s, I spent the better part of a month tracking them down—this for one of those marvelous, old-fashioned graduate school exercises that I hope students still undertake, at least on occasion. I stopped counting somewhere upward of 260. Had neither limitation of time nor lack of initiative intervened, I suspect I could have found many more, and the ensuing decades have produced editions no doubt by the score, such as the one you are reading now. They tend to proliferate during times of conspicuous social stress, such as the world wars. Does this pattern of publication disclose a desire to escape to nowhere during tumultuous times? Or perhaps to reflect on what a good place might be? Does it show an interest, felt if not explicitly contemplated, in the complexities of how to speak of social change?

We do well to read the text in more complex terms than as a blueprint to an ideal state. Its longer title—*On the Best Form of a Commonwealth and on the New Island of Utopia*—cues us into as much. The conjunction separates as well as joins the two parts. The "best form of a commonwealth," along with what it could mean to talk about and work toward it (dominant in Book 1), is not the same as the "new island of Utopia" (which dominates Book 2). After all, as Clarence Miller states in the introduction to this edition, few would want to live in such a regimented world as Hythloday describes. He even seems to forget a principle of justice that he urges. In his dialogue with Cardinal Morton, he argues convincingly that execution is an unjust and finally ineffectual punishment for thievery, but then in the description of his beloved isle, we learn that the Utopians practice capital punishment for a repeated offense of adultery (p. 99). Both offenses violate a biblical commandment (one the sixth, the other the seventh), so we might take this slip—criticism of one death sentence and implied praise of the other—as something of a wink from the author.

Something other is at stake here than a picture of a perfect world, which must exist elsewhere for More anyway. For this student of St. Augustine,[22] we work to better this world as best we can even when we know we'll fail. In *The City of God* (Bk. 15, chs. 1–6), Augustine locates the beginnings of the human city in the fratricide in which Cain kills Abel, and he makes the rather astute point that of the two, it is only Cain who builds a literal city. For a citizen of the City of God, life in this world is constant pilgrimage. It is thus fitting that, as several have pointed out, the life of Utopia is that of a monastery writ large.[23] Although the life of a monk traditionally involves staying home, the monastic way of renunciation reminds us that our lives are pilgrimage in a much deeper sense than locomotion can account for; the monk is one who uses the monastic rule to "follow the path to God."[24]

More wrote about the complications of forming an ideal commonwealth in this world, in a Latin poem titled *Quis Optimus Reipubae Status* ("What Is the Best Form of Government"), in which the speaker raises the question of which rules better, a senate or a king. He wrote the poem around the time he was composing *Utopia,* with which it appeared in 1518. Here the poem is rendered into English heroic couplets:

> Which one excels, a senate or a king?
> Likely the senate—it's a common thing:
> The best in greater numbers of the good.
> But how to find the numbers that you would?
> It's easier to hold one bad in view.
> A senate often lives between the two,
> But kings don't walk on any middle ground.
> Flawed senates may get counsel from the sound,
> But kings subdue the wisest of the earth.
> One is elected by the people. By birth
> The other reigns while holding in derision
> The whole of his subjected population.
> While greedy kings will chew their people up,
> An evil senate still leaves room for hope.
> The old tale says, Endure the sated pest;
> A hungry one invades, worse than the last.
> But greedy kings are never satisfied;
> A leech hangs on until the body's dried.
> Dissent will throw a senate into shambles.
> Not so the king, but that is where one gambles.
> When disagreement rules in weighty things . . .
> But hey, what started all this anyway?
> Are there people whom you hold in sway
> To shape their mode of rule? If so, you're king.

> Don't worry whether there would be abuse.
> Ask rather, Would it be of any use?[25]

Sure enough, Utopia is governed by a senate, but it was founded by a king (Utopus) who held sway to establish the system of rule and then legislated his position out of existence—an unlikely scenario, as things go in this world, and one that raises the question of whether democracy can be imposed on a people. It may be said of Utopus that, in taking on the role of king to create a system of democratic rule, the "latter end of his commonwealth forgets the beginning," as Antonio says of Gonzalo's ideal state.[26] The voice at the end of More's poem makes a similar point with the question "Would it be of any use?"

Given the ways of worldly power, could I escape—if I were king—the corrupting influence of my kingly position? How might one answer this question from More's point of view, given life in a fallen world of fallen people whose institutions are compromised by the effects of social sin,[27] where social justice falls by the wayside, and where the dangerous folly of the deluded rich and powerful holds sway more than the wise folly of the City of God (foolish in the eyes of this world) and what passes for wisdom and common sense is far too often the "common nonsense"[28] that arises from the distorting influence of our desires and fears, which are misshapen by life in a fallen world? Besides the corruptions of power, our struggles merely to survive compromise our desires to live well; as Lewis Mumford wrote, Utopia addresses the complication that "our attempts to live the good life are constantly perverted by our efforts to gain a living."[29] From Hythloday's point of view, the only solution is to establish Utopian institutions. But how do we get those institutions up and running? As Miller points out, they can be introduced only if they already exist.[30] You can't get there from here.

Utopia ushers its readers into a style of thought that confronts such complications as these. It is therefore advisable to attend to the style of this masterpiece of Neo-Latin prose. As Elizabeth McCutcheon points out, litotes—an affirmation formed by the negation of its opposite—plays no small part in More's text; she counted more than 140 instances in the Latin of the Yale edition. Because litotes does not do quite the same work as straightforward affirmation, it fosters a mindset that allows nuances and ambiguities otherwise easily glossed over, and thus encourages a habit of understanding in more complex terms than simple affirmation or negation accomplishes.[31] The figure of litotes is one of many that Stephen Greenblatt points to as forming the incongruous relationship between the two realms of the text—the world where the dialogue takes place and the island that Hythloday describes. Clearly, they are related, but their relationship is unstable and distorted.[32] One can even map out certain significant shifts in the style of Hythloday's sentences.[33] When he speaks of the injustices of his contemporary Europe, his sentences are of moderate length, similar to More's Latin prose in his other works. However, when Hythloday contrasts the real with his ideal, or describes the Utopians' simple way of life, he employs styles that represent "extremes that cannot be found anywhere else in More's Latin prose."[34] When contrasting the real with his ideal, he employs "marathon sentences" that go "beyond what ordinary Latin syntax can bear."[35] When describing his ideal, his sentences are simple and brief. Much of the meaning of the text depends on experience of its style, as of its shifts of style. Happily, Miller's translation preserves these stylistic features, and more.

Recognition of the need for a variety of styles and discourses was central to the humanist program. In *Utopia,* the character More emphasizes that there are many languages of truth. The language that a given speaker chooses should respond to the situation at hand and the persons addressed. Here he makes use of the metaphor of the world as a stage, arguably the most common of Renaissance commonplaces. As he says to Hythloday, "But there is another sort of philosophy better suited to public affairs. It knows its role and adapts to it, keeping to its part in the play at hand with harmony and decorum" (p. 43). The Latin of this passage even refers literally to the boards of the theater, the stage (*scaena*). We may be reminded of the anecdote, related by More's son-in-law, about the future Lord Chancellor: during his apprenticeship in the home of Archbishop Morton, where "though [More] was young of years, yet would he at Christmas-tide suddenly sometimes step in among the players, and never studying for the matter, make a part of his own there presently among them, which made the lookers-on more sport than all the players beside."[36] The humanist spirit recognized that the stage of the world demands improvisation with many language styles.

It may seem curious that More speaks of this theatrical metaphor as a philosophy.[37] But there is a way of understanding ourselves and our world implicit in the metaphor and its relationship to the arts of rhetoric, one that includes a variety of roles and language worlds by means of which humans negotiate experience. One term for this way of understanding is what has been styled relationism.[38] Because everything is related to everything else, there is no singular statement to make about anything. Further, because every statement (such as the one I am making now) conceals as much as it reveals, any statement, no matter how true, must be supplemented by other statements. There is no final word, as there is no final interpretation. What makes a given utterance relevant has everything to do with the situation within which it is made, who is speaking, and who is addressed. None of this is to say that humans cannot know something true—were this the case, we could not know it—but rather that there is no absolute human perspective or singular language of truth, as Hythloday insists that there is.[39]

Given this relationist style of thinking, we may discern in the humanists' work early stirrings toward what Bernard Lonergan identified in his aptly titled "The Transition from a Classicist World-View to Historical-Mindedness."[40] This transition moves from a monolithic understanding of what it means to be human to the insight that there is a great variety of valid ways to be human, as there is a great variety of valid languages of knowing. The *Utopia* suggests that we are permitted to reflect on how we might change our institutions, revise our social structures, conduct our cultural and civic lives differently. For all of its monolithic structure and faceless anonymity, even Utopia is permeable to outside influence—Utopians eagerly learn Greek, printing, and papermaking (pp. 92–95). Reading *Utopia* means entering into a dialogue, with oneself and others, that continues to this day.[41]

Another influence on the emerging historical-mindedness of More's era was the ongoing exploration of the globe, as learning about the varieties of culture beyond Europe enabled a greater appreciation of the forms that human societies, and everyday human life, can take. Hythloday himself accompanied Amerigo Vespucci on three of his voyages. Accounts of these journeys provide descriptions of peoples with striking similarities to the Utopians. Thus, we learn of a society in which, as in Utopia, women accompany men into battle, an Epicurean sensibility reigns, and people "hold their habitations in common."[42] Perhaps most striking is the attitude toward gold and other objects that pass for wealth in Europe: "They do not value gold, nor pearls, nor gems, nor such other things as we consider precious here in Europe."[43] The description calls immediately to mind the Utopians' use of gold for chamber pots and shackles, as well as the marvelous anecdote of the Anemolian ambassadors (pp. 76–78).

Of all the questions that surround *Utopia,* the most vexing has been that of More's attitude toward common ownership of property. Character More objects to the Utopians' community of goods. Even so, it is difficult to ignore the forceful language that he assigns to Hythloday in defense of common property:

> . . . it seems to me that wherever there is private property, where everything is measured in terms of money, it is hardly ever possible for the common good to be served with justice and prosperity, unless you think justice is served when all the best things go to the worst people or that happiness is possible when everything is shared among very few, who themselves are not entirely happy, while the rest are plunged into misery. (p. 46)

But character More responds that private ownership is necessary as a goad, for the promise of profit motivates people to work, and too many are lazy louts without the promise of one day owning their own demesne, no matter how small. After the account of Utopian life, he intervenes again, this time with the contention that community of goods "entirely undermines all nobility, magnificence, splendor, and majesty, which are (in the popular view) the true adornments and ornaments of a commonwealth" (p. 134). The appeal to the "popular view" might raise an eyebrow or two, for More remained throughout his life critical of general opinion as a source of wisdom, as did his friend Erasmus, whose *Praise of Folly* tells the tale. We do well to bear in mind that it was More's critical stance with regard to the popular position that got him imprisoned and killed in the end.

A further complication in considering the Utopians' community of goods is its prominence in the traditions that More revered. Thus, in Plato's *Republic*—which casts a long shadow over More's text—common ownership is a way of life for the Guardian class, part of the training in virtue for those who are to lead and protect. Then all we need do is shift from Athens to Jerusalem to read the second chapter of the great chronicle of the early Christian communities, Acts of the Apostles, to discover that the believers "held everything in common, and they sold their belongings and possessions and divided them to all according as anyone had need" (2:44–45). This is similar to what Hythloday has done—divided up his possessions among relatives and friends—thus freeing himself for a philosophic life (p. 15). More would have known some echo of the early believers' community of possessions during the four years he lived as a guest of the Carthusians at their Charterhouse in London.[44] This sharing of goods was a well-established part of monastic tradition; the "vice of private ownership must be uprooted from the monastery," St. Benedict wrote.[45] Closer to the composition of *Utopia,* Erasmus included in his Adagia "*Amicorum communia omnia*" ("Among friends all is held in common"). In the 1515 edition, Erasmus gave this adage pride of place at the opening of the collection, stating, "Since there is nothing more wholesome or more generally accepted than this proverb, it seemed good to place it as a favourable omen at the head of this collection of adages."[46] Kathy Eden takes this three-word Latin adage as her point of departure in a marvelous book-length study of Erasmus and the humanists.[47]

One of the more nuanced treatments of common ownership occurs in St. Thomas Aquinas's *Summa Theologiae.*[48] Although Aquinas is sometimes associated with the scholastic philosophy against which the humanists inveighed, they generally regarded him not as a scholastic philosopher, but rather as a theologian and Doctor (that is, teacher) of the church. On the one hand, Aquinas set out three reasons why private ownership is helpful to human life: (1) it provides motivation to work; (2) it allows for orderliness in human affairs; and (3) it enables peaceful social relations (ST 2–2ae, Q. 66, A. 2). All three of these accord with the views that character More espouses. On the other hand, in describing humans' fundamental relationship to the world, Aquinas articulates a vision of communal possession:

> Community of goods is ascribed to the natural law, not that the natural law dictates that all things should be possessed in common and that nothing should be possessed as one's own: but because the division of possessions is not according to the natural law, but rather arose from human agreement which belongs to positive law, as stated above. (Q. 57, AA. 2–3)

Hence, private ownership is not incompatible with natural law, which also does not require it; rather, private ownership is an "addition thereto devised by human reason" (2–2ae, Q. 66, A. 2, Reply to Objection 1). The natural law recognizes that humans hold all the world in common. Private ownership is merely a provisional, pragmatic, and contingent means whereby humans make creative use of what is fundamentally communal. One valid reading of the *Utopia* sees the proposition concerning community of property as a way of loosening the metaphysical grip on ownership, reminding readers that we own things in this world merely by convention, not by nature.

If Aquinas had lived in the twentieth century—a speculation I may be allowed given the fictive space of utopian writing—he might have joined with Paul Ricoeur in considering utopian thought alongside ideology. A working definition of ideology, cast in Thomistic terms, is the taking of the provisional and pragmatic for the metaphysical. Thus, stating a right to private ownership as a metaphysical given is an example of the false consciousness wherein Ricoeur finds ideology to function. In his reading, the best function of utopian thinking is as an antidote to ideology, for such thinking provides an opportunity to play one's identity out and away from the prison house of the here and now. As he put it, "This function of utopia is finally the function of the nowhere. To be here, *Da-sein,* I must also be able to be nowhere."[49] Utopian thought relates to identity because part of identity is prospective, who and what we desire and strive to be—"What we call ourselves is also what we expect and yet what we are not."[50] But ideology and utopia will not remain separate;[51] they tend to interweave, and one issue worth further reflection is how

157

the two function together as well as tend to tear apart, in *Utopia* and elsewhere.

Up for further consideration too is the place of this text in the trajectories of human consciousness in the tumultuous times of the early modern era. As already adverted to, part of the humanist movement related to shifts in awareness emerging from exploration of the planet. But other forces figured into these alterations also. One of these was the introduction of print (an innovation that the Utopians took to, as Hythloday witnesses). Working just after the incunabulum—or cradle—of print, the humanists were perhaps the first generation of European writers fully to embrace this technology, an important part of the era's seismic shifts in thinking and sensibility.[52] As one scholar put it, "As an institution the printing press represented an autonomous and cosmopolitan site for the production of knowledge free of lay and ecclesiastical control."[53] Print, in other words, helped to create a new kind of imaginative space, and a new feel for how intellection happens. The printed book or pamphlet allows an impression of a free-floating island of discourse, and even though no discourse is ever really broken off from the dialogues taking place in the human lifeworld, print technology was related (though not reducible) to new ways, including more cosmopolitan and mobile ways, of imagining and conducting intellectual life. Like Cardinal Morton breaking into the speech of the ponderous lawyer (p. 26), the discourse emergent with print disrupted older styles. These changes also created tensions. Hanan Yoran has gone perhaps as far as anyone in showing the discursive tensions of *Utopia*. As he points out, nearly all symbolic action has been eliminated from this island, where even law—that most contentiously symbol-laden of realms—is fantasized into a commonsense reign of the obvious (p. 102). For a community of scholars to whom all of human life is interwoven with symbolic action, such a space as this is a no-place indeed.[54] The ways in which print technology figured into these tensions, along with the creative possibilities it allowed, might be further scanned.[55]

Another area for further study is the family resemblance between *Utopia*, along with humanist discourse generally, and certain strains of postmodern thought. With their emphases on the performativity of human identity, the slipperiness of language, and the provisionality of all human discourses—along with their commitment to literary experimentation and serious engagement in play—the humanists may be taken in some ways as precursors to Derrida and company.[56] While the early humanists were far from deconstructionists avant la lettre, they could nevertheless have appreciated Derrida's assertion that when it comes to philosophical statement, political discourse, or ethical judgment, negotiation is always necessary, and there is always something about negotiation that "gets one's hands dirty" even when one is negotiating "in the name of purity."[57] More was in Flanders busy with negotiations when the opportunity to write *Utopia* fell into his soiled hands.

After Hythloday's description of Utopia, character More says to the reader, but not to Hythloday, that he harbors some objections to the Utopian way of life. He would prefer at this point, however, to avoid contention, so instead of arguing, he extends a hand to Hythloday: "I took his hand and led him in to dinner, though first I said we would have another time to consider these matters more thoroughly and to confer more fully. I only wish this would happen someday!" (p. 134). The narrative comes to its close with this gesture of friendship and a prospective note, the desire to talk more fully at some unspecified time in the future. Even with his objections, his final sentence—prospective as well—ends the text with wistful agreement, as he states, "I readily confess that in the Utopian commonwealth are very many features which in our societies I would wish rather than expect to see" (p. 135). Let us confer, then, so that we may discover what event may yet arrive out of that nowhere that is the future.[58]

Introduction

1. J. H. Hexter argues in *More's Utopia: The Biography of an Idea* (Princeton: Princeton University Press, 1952) and in Edward Surtz, S.J., and J. H. Hexter, eds., *Utopia,* vol. 4 of *The Complete Works of St. Thomas More* (New Haven: Yale University Press, 1965), pp. xv–xxiii, that because there are biographical details about the speaker of Book 2 that fit the Hythloday of Book 1, the opening of Book 1 up to the point where Giles asks Hythloday why he does not serve a prince must have also been written in Flanders. He also argues that the passionate peroration of Book 2, in which Hythloday excoriates Europe and defends communism, was written in London. However probable or plausible Hexter's arguments are, More could have written all of Book 1 in London, adding biographical details in Book 2 and possibly its peroration after he finished Book 1.

2. The term "dystopia" had to be invented to accommodate the negative features of More's fantasy.

3. *Utopia,* with an introduction and notes by Edward Surtz, S.J. (New Haven: Yale University Press, 1964), p. xxvi.

4. In my translation I have tried to reproduce stylistic elements of *Utopia* as well as its meaning. I have borrowed and modified some passages from my article "Style and Meaning in *Utopia:* Hythloday's Sentences and Diction."

5. " 'Si Hythlodaeo Credimus': Vision and Revision in Thomas More's *Utopia,*" *Soundings* (formerly *The Christian Scholar*) 51 (1968): 271–89; reprinted in *Essential Articles for the Study of Thomas More,* ed. Richard S. Sylvester and Germain Marc'hadour (Hamden, Conn.: Archon Books, 1977), pp. 290–301 (p. 298).

7. How the other capital sins survive in the absence of pride and just which of the other capital sins cause the crimes punished by the Utopians are also difficult questions.

8. Valerian Paget's *More's Millennium* (1909) was simply a modernization of Robinson's translation and has no independent value.

9. The translation in the Yale edition (Surtz and Hexter, eds., 1965) was a reworking of Richards' translation by Edward Surtz, but the result was usually not an improvement.

Utopia

1. More had been undersheriff since September 3, 1510. As such he presided over the court at one of the sheriff's jails, where he heard various (mostly minor) cases.

2. The poem, "by the Poet Laureate Anemolius," was probably written by More himself. On the name Anemolius, see note 186, below.

3. In the first edition (Louvain, 1516) and in the running heads of the two Basel editions of 1518, this letter is described as a "preface."

4. Peter Giles (c. 1486–1533) was a humanist friend of More and Erasmus. He was a corrector at the press of Dirk Martens in his native city of Antwerp and was a clerk of that city from 1512 on.

5. The name "Utopia" derives from Greek *ou* ("not") and *topos* ("place"), meaning "no place" (More also called it by the equivalent Latin name "nusquama"). "Utopia" includes a pun because the initial "u" may also be derived from Greek *eu* ("good"). Hence Utopia is a good place which is no place.

6. More visited Giles in Antwerp in September 1515; together with a letter dated 3 September 1516, he sent the manuscript of *Utopia* to Erasmus for publication.

7. The angel Raphael is a saving guide and healer in the biblical book of Tobias. Raphael's surname, Hythloday, is derived from Greek words meaning "peddler of nonsense."

8. More refers to the principal divisions of rhetoric according to the classical tradition: invention (finding matter), disposition (arranging it), and eloquence (stylistic elaboration).

9. This description applies to most of Hythloday's description of Utopia itself, but hardly to the elaborate and often passionate eloquence of Hythloday's language in much of Book 1 and in his peroration at the

end of Book 2. Almost nothing in this letter (or in *Utopia* itself, for that matter) can be taken at face value.

10. More describes himself (accurately) as devoted to the active life which Hythloday rejects.

11. John Clement (c. 1500–1572), one of the first students at Colet's humanist school, St. Paul's, became a page and pupil in More's household about 1514; later he became a distinguished physician.

12. "Anyder" is coined from the Greek for "waterless"; "Amaurot" from the Greek for "made dark or dim."

13. Sidenote: *Note the theological distinction between lying and speaking a falsehood.* Though it is apparently not found among the theologians, the distinction between *mentiri* (tell a lie) and *mendacium dicere* (speak a falsehood, with no intention of deceiving) derives from Aulus Gellius (11.11.1–4) and was well known. Erasmus, and perhaps Peter Giles, probably added the sidenotes that appeared in the margins of the original edition.

14. Sidenote: *A holy ambition!*

15. Sidenote: *Human judgments are ungrateful.*

16. Sidenote: *Persons with no "nose"* [appreciation of wit] *he calls "flat-nosed."*

17. Sidenote: *A saying.* See Erasmus, *Adages* 293 in *The Collected Works of Erasmus* (Toronto: University of Toronto Press, 1974–), vol. 31, p. 311. *The Collected Works of Erasmus* is hereinafter referred to as *CWE*, followed by the volume number in italic and the page number in roman type: *CWE 31*, 311.

18. The metaphor seems to be drawn from wrestling.

19. Sidenote: *A remarkable comparison.*

20. Erasmus, *Adages* 28 (*CWE 31*, 76–77).

21. In August 1513 Henry's army had been victorious at the Battle of the Spurs and briefly occupied Thérouanne and Tournai; but his French campaigns, then and later, were as futile and destructive as those of the French kings in Italy.

22. The difficulties were mainly connected with the wool trade between England and Flanders. They were serious enough for Wolsey to be worried early in 1515 that Charles would seize the English fleet for back taxes.

23. By 1515 Charles V, later Holy Roman Emperor (1519), was Duke of Burgundy and Prince of Castile.

24. Sidenote: *Cuthbert Tunstall.* Tunstall (1474–1559), bishop of London (1522) and later Durham (1530), was a close friend whom More admired throughout his lifetime. On 12 May 1516 Tunstall became Master of the Rolls and Vice-chancellor; as such he was chief of the twelve assistants to the Lord Chancellor.

25. Sidenote: *An adage.* See Erasmus, *Adages* 1406–7 (*CWE 33*, 245).

26. Jean (or perhaps Jacques) de Halewyn, Seigneur de Maldeghem.

27. De Themsecke (d. ca. 1536), a doctor of the law and a member of Charles V's council at Mechlin, was employed on many diplomatic missions. (Cassel is now in northern France.)

28. On or before 25 July 1515.

29. Sidenote: *Peter Giles.* In Flemish his name is "Gillis" or "Gilles," but the usual English translation of his Latin name ("Aegidius") is "Giles."

30. Giles (1486–1533) was learned in the law and edited classical and humanist works. Since 1512 he had been chief clerk of the court of justice at Antwerp.

31. Cf. Matt. 10:16. The same combination was part of the printer's mark of Johann Froben, who printed the two 1518 editions of *Utopia.*

32. More left England 12 May 1515.

33. Palinurus, Aeneas' steersman, dozed at the helm, fell overboard, and drowned (*Aeneid* 5.833–61), unlike the alert Odysseus and observant Plato who learned much from their travels (*Odyssey* 1.1–4; Diogenes Laertius 3.6–7.18–22).

34. More expressed the same opinion in his *Letter to Oxford,* in *The Complete Works of St. Thomas More,* vol. 15, ed. Daniel Kinney (New Haven: Yale University Press, 1986), p. 143. (Works in this series are hereinafter cited as *CWM,* followed by the volume number in italic and the page number in roman type: *CWM 15*, 143).

35. In 1515 the Portuguese excelled in exploration, especially in the far east.

36. The voyages (1503–4) of the Florentine explorer Amerigo Vespucci (1451–1512), who was in the employ of the King of Portugal, were described in two Latin narratives (of disputed authenticity) published about 1507; one of the versions mentions the twenty-four mariners left behind in a fort at the farthest point of the voyage (Cape Frio in southeast Brazil).

37. Lucan, *Pharsalia* 7.818–19; cf. Augustine, *City of God* 1.12.

38. Sidenote: *Apophthem;* cf. Erasmus, *Apophthegmata* 7, Anaxagoras Clazomenus 4, and Cicero, *Tusculan Disputations* 1.43.104.

39. The Portuguese had visited Calicut (a city on the west coast of India, not Calcutta) by 1487 and established a station there in 1511.

40. This is not an ordinary bench covered with sod. The small woodcut of the scene in the two editions of 1518 shows that it was a long wooden box filled with earth and covered on top with growing grass.

41. The torrid zone between the Tropic of Cancer and the Tropic of Capricorn, the northern and southern limits between which the sun's orbit was thought to move.

42. Scylla was a six-headed sea monster (*Odyssey* 12.73–100, 234–59; *Aeneid* 3.424–32); Celaeno was one of the harpies, disgusting birds with women's faces (*Aeneid* 3.209–58); the Laestrigonians were giant cannibals (*Odyssey* 10.17–133).

43. It seems likely that at this point More inserted the bulk of Book 1, the dialogue about counseling kings, which was written after Book 2, when More had returned to London. (See the Introduction, p. vii, and p. 141n.1.) In this addition More does not limit himself to describing Utopian institutions but gives Raphael's narration about the Polylerites, Achorians, and Macarians.

44. Hythloday paraphrases a definition of liberty given by Cicero in a context similar to this one (*De officiis* 1.20.69–70).

45. Cf. Erasmus, *Adages* 115, 121, 3064 (*CWE 31,* 158–60, 167–68).

46. A Cornish rebellion was crushed at the Battle of Blackheath on 22 June 1497.

47. More had admired Morton (1420–1500) since the time he was a page in his household (c. 1490–92). He is portrayed as skilled and shrewd in More's *Richard III* (*CWM 2,* 90–92).

48. In his *Description of England* (1587), ed. Georges Edelen (Ithaca, N.Y.: Cornell University Press, 1968), p. 87, William Harrison reported that in the reign of Henry VIII alone 72,000 thieves and vagabonds were hanged.

49. Since Hythloday was in England in late 1497 and early 1498 he may be referring to English skirmishes in France in the early 1490s. But as he speaks in 1515, he may also be thinking of the much heavier casualties in Henry VIII's futile French campaigns of 1512–13.

50. Plato uses the figure of the drones to describe an oligarchy ruled by rich men who exploit the poor and contribute nothing to society (*Republic* 8.552B–C).

51. The parallel between soldiers and robbers is a frequent theme among humanists; see, for example, Erasmus, *Complaint of Peace* (*CWE 27*, 317).

52. In the time of Francis I the French relied mostly on Swiss and German mercenaries.

53. The Latin "morosophi" (transliterated from Greek) means literally "foolish wisemen" (the reverse of the modern "sophomore"). See Lucian, *Alexander* 40. Erasmus uses it in *The Praise of Folly*, tr. Clarence H. Miller (New Haven: Yale University Press, 1979), p. 13; in *De copia, Opera omnia* 1.12C; and in *Adagia* (prol., *CWE 31*, 23).

54. *Bellum Catalinae* 16.3.

55. Foreign mercenaries often wreaked havoc in France during the Hundred Years' War (1337–1453).

56. The Greek historian Herodian (mentioned in Book 2 as one of the authors Hythloday brought to Utopia) describes how several emperors were murdered by the barbarian mercenaries of the Praetorian guard. After the first Punic War, foreign mercenaries revolted against their Carthaginian employers. From the thirteenth to the sixteenth century, the Mamelukes (originally mercenaries from Turkey and Circassia) ruled despotically a large empire consisting of Egypt, Syria, and other parts of the Middle East.

57. Especially Italy, which was often devastated by foreign mercenaries; Machiavelli, who firmly opposed the use of mercenaries, gives many examples of the harm they caused.

58. The English defeated the French decisively at Crécy (1346), Poitiers (1356), and Agincourt (1415).

59. Between the thirteenth and eighteenth centuries, much arable land was enclosed by hedges or ditches and used to pasture sheep. Hythloday's arguments against enclosure were widespread, and though it had its supporters (mostly because of the profitability of the wool trade), it undoubtedly caused much suffering to farm laborers and destroyed many villages.

60. Long before and after 1515 many sumptuary laws were passed against extravagant display, especially in clothing, but they were honored more in the breach than the observance.

61. During the reigns of Henry VII and Henry VIII laws were passed forbidding gaming and alehouses, limiting enclosure, restoring land from pasture to tillage, and restricting monopolies, but with little effect.

62. Sidenote: *This shows the Cardinal's usual way of interrupting anyone who talks too much.*

63. A proverbial saying (Erasmus, *Adages* 924), derived primarily from Cicero, *De officiis* 1.10.33.

64. Sidenote: *Manlian edicts from Livy.* Proverbial for "harshly unjust" (Erasmus, *Adages* 987). The Roman consul Manlius executed his son for winning a victory without having permission to do so (Livy 8.7.1–22).

65. Stoics such as Zeno, Seneca, and Epictetus believed that virtue consisted in ignoring exterior forces and remaining faithful to the interior dictates of reason about what is right; such faithfulness has no degrees but is either kept or not. Cicero presents and refutes the paradox in *De finibus* 4.10.21–23; Horace ridicules it in *Satires* 1.3.113–24.

66. Exod. 20:13, Deut. 5:17. (All scriptural references are to the Vulgate text and numbering.)

67. Exod. 22:1–4.

68. The Mosaic law does, of course, prescribe death as a punishment for various crimes. And even under the more merciful Christian dispensation, Hythloday does not always condemn capital punishment; as the remedy of last resort, it is employed by the Polylerites and the Utopians (pp. 30, 99).

69. A name formed from Greek *polus* ("much") and *leros* ("nonsense").

70. Sidenote: *We should note this, since we do otherwise.* Erasmus expresses the same opinion in *The Education of a Christian Prince* (*CWE 27,* 270).

71. Sidenote: *But nowadays the servants of noblemen find such a haircut attractive.*

72. Erasmus, *Adages* 1612.

73. If a criminal could reach a place of asylum or sanctuary (usually a church) he could not be arrested, though during the reign of Henry VII the privilege was discussed and somewhat curtailed. It is debated in More's *Richard III* (*CWM 2,* 27–33).

74. Sidenote: *An entertaining exchange between a friar and a fool.*

75. Cf. Erasmus, *Adages* 113 (*CWE 31,* 154–55).

76. Sidenote: *A proverb frequently bandied about among beggars.* There seems to be no recorded or recognized proverb here (though it might still have been a frequent saying among beggars); there may be some allusion to the priest who passed by the wounded Samaritan (Luke 10:31).

77. Unordained members of religious orders were called "lay brothers."

78. Sidenote: *He alludes to the Horatian phrase "doused with Italian vinegar."* See *Satires* 1.7.32 and Erasmus, *Adages* 1252 (*CWE 33*, 164). The phrase is here translated as "needled."

79. John 17:12, 2 Thess. 2:3.

80. Luke 21:19.

81. Ps. 4:5. Sidenote: *How well the people in the story speak in character!*

82. Ps. 68:10.

83. Sidenote: *Apparently the friar, in his ignorance, misuses "zelus" as if it were neuter like "scelus."* In 4 Kings 2:23–25 some children mocked Elisha because of his baldness; when he cursed them two bears came out of the woods and tore forty-two of them to pieces. The friar quotes a hymn attributed to Adam of St. Victor, sung within the octave of Easter. In the ordinary pronunciation of Erasmus' time *zelus* ("zeal") could sound like *scelus* ("crime"). The confusion produces the following result: those who mocked Elisha . . . feel the crime of the bald man.

84. Prov. 26:5. But the preceding verse says: "Do not answer the fool according to his folly lest you become like him."

85. Perhaps alluding to Ps. 7:16.

86. *Republic* 5.473C–D, *Epistles* 7.326A–B.

87. During his three sojourns at Syracuse, Plato failed in his attempt to reform the tyrant Dionysius or his son (also Dionysius); see his *Epistles* 7 and Plutarch, *Dion.* 4.1–5.3, 10.1–20.2.

88. Here Hythloday launches into a 464-word sentence, suspended, unrealistically intricate, interminable (as Lupton called it), which ends with "react to this speech." Though translators (with the exception of Robinson) have generally broken up this sentence to make it easier, such manipulation is unjustified: the sentence is no easier in Latin than in English. Its difficulty springs from Hythloday's difficult outlook.

89. In 1515, the time of More's imagined interview with Hythloday, the king of France was Francis I, who continued the policy of his predecessors Charles VII and Louis XII. All three invented claims to

Milan and Naples, but their military adventures in Italy foundered in confusion and intrigue.

90. The French won Milan in 1499, lost it in 1512, regained it in 1515. They won Naples in 1495, lost it in 1496, regained it in 1501, and lost it in 1503.

91. Sidenote: *Indirectly he is discouraging the French from acquiring Italy.* At the battle of Agnadello (1509), France defeated Venice and deprived it of its territory on the mainland. By 1515, when the Venetians helped Francis I in his campaign again Milan, the French king restored Verona to his Venetian ally. Hythloday wonders if the French king is ready to turn on his recent ally once more.

92. After the death of Charles the Rash, Duke of Burgundy (1477), Louis XI of France tried to seize all the vast Burgundian holdings, though many parts clearly did not belong to France.

93. The German mercenary footsoldiers were surpassed only by the Swiss; both were despised and excoriated by Erasmus and many humanists.

94. Emperor Maximilian of Hapsburg, grandfather of Charles V, was usually impecunious and totally unreliable. A votive offering was normally an expensive gift left in a church or shrine in thanksgiving for a favor from God or a saint.

95. With the help of troops sent by a duped Henry VIII, Ferdinand II, King of Aragon and regent of Castile, occupied southern Navarre in 1512 and annexed it to Castile in 1515.

96. Charles V, prince of Castile and the future emperor (1519) was often affianced for dynastic reasons, especially to French brides.

97. Francis I did make a treaty with England in April 1515.

98. The Scots were traditionally allies of France against England.

99. The French had supported several pretenders to the English throne during the reigns of Henry VII and Henry VIII: Lambert Simnel, Perkin Warbeck, Edmund de la Pole, and his brother Richard.

100. Erasmus, *Adages* 860 (*CWE 32*, 215).

101. Cf. More's epigram "On Lust for Power": "Among many kings there will be scarcely one, if there is really one, who is satisfied to have one kingdom. And yet among many kings there will be scarcely one, if there is really one, who rules a single kingdom well" (*CWM 3/2*, 257).

102. Sidenote: *A notable example.* From Greek *a-* ("without") and *choros* ("place, country").

103. More here echoes Erasmus' *Adages* 1401 (*CWE 33*, 237–43): "Sparta is your portion; make it flourish."

104. Hythloday presents his second imaginary council in an even longer marathon sentence (926 words); it is just as extravagant in Latin as in this English translation.

105. Fraudulent manipulation of the currency was practiced by Edward IV, Henry VII, and (later) Henry VIII.

106. In 1492 Henry VII not only levied taxes for a pretended war against France but accepted a bribe from Charles VIII of France for not fighting it.

107. Henry VII's ministers Empson and Dudley were notorious for such chicanery.

108. The royal prerogative, the special, inherited claims of the king apart from common law, was a subject of considerable dispute even in More's time, though it became more heated in the following century.

109. Hythloday adapts Cicero's statement in *De officiis* 1.8.25: "Recently Marcus Crassus said that no amount of money is enough for one who wishes to be head of state unless it produces enough income to maintain an army."

110. Among the techniques mentioned by Aristotle by which tyrants maintain their power are keeping subjects poor and humble-spirited and pretending to rule for the advantage of the citizens (*Politics* 5.9.4, 8, 11, 1313b, 1314a–b).

111. The biblical and Homeric figure of kings as shepherds was widespread; in his speech at the opening of Parliament in 1529 More compared kings to shepherds. See also his Latin epigrams against tyranny (*CWM 3/2*, 162–65, 168–69).

112. The saying derives from Manlius Curius Dentatus (Plutarch, *Moralia* 194F) but it was also attributed to Gaius Fabricius Luscinus by classical and medieval authors.

113. From the Greek *makarios* ("happy"); the Greek word introduces each of the beatitudes (Matt. 5:3–11).

114. More may be thinking of Henry VII, who had an enormous sum in his treasury when he died.

115. Sidenote: *A proverb.* See Erasmus, *Adages* 1387 (*CWE 31*, 376).

116. The following argument centers on the moral and rhetorical notion of decorum (Cicero, *De officiis* 1.27.93–39.141, *Orator* 21.69–22.74,

and *De oratore* 3.55.109–12). It is also based on the conflict between rhetorical persuasion, which deals with probable truths, and philosophical logic, which produces demonstrable truths.

117. Sidenote: *The philosophy of the schools.* In the text and sidenote this philosophy is designated "scholastica." The only academic philosophy in More's time was that of the universities, which we nowadays call scholasticism, so that in this case "academic" and "scholastic" are practically synonymous. The humanists generally attacked the hairsplitting excesses of scholastic philosophy and favored a more rhetorical approach to literature and life. See, for example, More's *Letter to Dorp* (*CWM 15*, 29–39, 49–70).

118. Sidenote: *A marvelous comparison. Octavia* is a tragedy once attributed to Seneca in which Seneca discusses the abuse of power with Nero. Cf. Erasmus, *Adages* 91, "to be subservient to your role" (*CWE 31*, 131–32).

119. Sidenote [in Greek]: *A mute role.* John Clement plays such a part in *Utopia.*

120. Plato allows rulers (even presumably philosopher-kings) to lie to their subjects for a useful purpose (*Republic* 3.21.414B–415D, 5.8.459C–D). Quintilian says that "everyone must allow, what even the sternest of the Stoics admit, that the good man will sometimes tell a lie" (*Institutes* 12.1.38).

121. Matt. 10:27, Luke 12:3.

122. The so-called Lesbian ruler was made of lead so as to accommodate itself to measuring curved surfaces; see Erasmus, *Adages* 493 (*CWE 31*, 465).

123. *Adelphoe* 1.2.145–47.

124. *Republic* 6.10.496D–E.

125. See p. 101.

126. According to Diogenes Laertius (3.23), "the Arcadians and Thebans, when they were founding Megalopolis, invited Plato to be their legislator; but . . . when he discovered that they were opposed to equality of possessions, he refused to go." In the *Republic* Plato prescribes community of property (and of wives and children) only for the guardians (5.12.464B–E), but in the *Laws* he says that in the best state it would be observed by the whole populace (5.739B–D).

127. More summarizes Aristotle's arguments in the *Politics* (2.1.2.1260b–

4.13.1267b) against Plato's advocacy of communism. Aristotle's arguments had been adopted by the medieval scholastics such as Thomas Aquinas in his commentary on Aristotle's *Politics* (2.1–7).

128. The numerical equivalents of the Greek letters in "Abraxas" (the usual form, rather than "Abraxa") add up to 365. The name was given to the highest of the 365 heavens invented by the heretic Basilides.

129. Sidenote: *A greater task than cutting through the Isthmus.* Several attempts to dig a canal across the Isthmus of Corinth failed so that the attempt became proverbial for failure (Erasmus, *Adages* 3326).

130. Sidenote: *Common effort lightens a burden.*

131. According to Erasmus, in Utopia More "represented the English commonwealth in particular" (*CWE* 7, 23.281). In 1587, according to William Harrison's *Description of England* (1587), ed. Georges Edelen (Cornell University Press, 1968, pp. 86–87), England had fifty-three counties, which, together with London, make it match the city-states of Utopia. The city-states are mostly independent but loosely federated, each having its own governor; they are united only by codes and customs, as well as a triennial meeting of a senate.

132. Sidenote: *Likeness breeds concord.*

133. Sidenote: *But such a desire is the curse of modern commonwealths.*

134. From a Greek compound meaning "ruler of a tribe."

135. Pliny mentions artificial incubation (*Natural History* 10.76.154–55) but it seems not to have been practiced in More's time.

136. That is, they do not use it to make beer or ale, as the English do.

137. Sidenote: *The advantage of communal labor.*

138. From a Greek adjective meaning "without water." Amaurot resembles London in its tidal river (the Thames) and smaller stream (Fleet Ditch, except that London's stream was foul and unpleasant).

139. Sidenote: *The same thing happens to the Thames in England.*

140. Sidenote: *In this feature London is also like Amaurot.* But Amaurot has the advantage of having its bridge above the city, not below it.

141. Sidenote: *This is reminiscent of Plato.* See *Republic* 3.22.416D.

142. Sidenote: *Virgil also praised the usefulness of gardens.* See *Georgics* 4.116–48.

143. That is, 244 B.C., when Aegis IV became king of Sparta; he was killed because of the egalitarian reforms he wished to introduce. See Richard Schoeck, "More, Plutarch, and King Aegis: Spartan History and the Meaning of History," *Philological Quarterly* 35 (1956): 366–

75; reprinted in *Essential Articles for the Study of Thomas More,* ed. Richard Sylvester and Germain Marc'hadour (Hamden, Conn.: Archon Books, 1977), pp. 275–80.

144. In More's time lead was commonly used to roof important buildings. William Harrison, in his *Description of England* (1587), ed. Georges Edelen (Ithaca, N.Y.: Cornell University Press, 1968), speaks of "fine alabaster burned, which they call plaster of Paris, whereof in some places we have great plenty and that very profitable against the rage of fire," but he is describing the plastering of interior walls, not roofs, which he says are covered with shingles, straw, sedge, reeds, or slate (p. 196).

145. Glass windows were uncommon in homes during More's time; oiled linen, sheets of horn, or lattices of wicker or wood were used instead. Hythloday means that oiled linen is brighter and more impervious than linen alone, not that it is superior to glass.

146. Sidenote: *In the Utopian language "tranibor" means "chief director."* "Syphogrant" seems to be derived from the Greek compound meaning "wise old man" (or perhaps "old man of the sty" = steward). "Tranibor" seem to come from a Greek compound meaning "plain eater." But other meanings have also been suggested. In fact, Hythloday continues to use the older terms "syphogrant" and "tranibor," not "phylarch" (ruler of a tribe) or "protophylarch" (chief phylarch).

147. Thus there are six thousand families in Utopia, excluding the countryside (see p. 54).

148. Sidenote: *A remarkable way of electing officials.*

149. Sidenote: *Tyranny is hateful to the well-ordered commonwealth.*

150. Utopia is a federation of democratic republics: the households elect the syphogrants, who elect the tranibors and governor (whom they can also remove from office). The syphogrants also select the class of scholars, from which all high officials are chosen.

151. Sidenote: *Disputes should be settled quickly, but nowadays they are deliberately and lengthily prolonged.*

152. Sidenote: *Nothing should be decided hastily.*

153. But for the whole island of Utopia there is no single executive branch to carry out or enforce the deliberations or decisions of this council.

154. Sidenote: *Would that the same thing were done in our councils.*

155. Sidenote: *This is the meaning of the proverb "take counsel at night."* See Erasmus, *Adages 1143* (*CWE 33,* 96).

156. Sidenote: *Farming is an occupation common to everyone, though here it is fobbed off on a few despised workers.*

157. Plato (*Republic* 7.797A–B) and Aristotle (*Politics* 7.15.5.1336a). Plato specifically advises that "to make a good farmer [a man] must play [in childhood] at tilling land" (*Republic* 1.643B–C).

158. Sidenote: *Trades should be learned to satisfy needs, not luxury.*

159. Sidenote: *Let everyone learn the trade for which he has a natural aptitude.*

160. Unlike the Utopians, Plato insists that each craftsman must have only one trade (*Republic* 2.11.370A–C, 2.13.474B–C; *Laws* 8.846D–E).

161. Sidenote: *The idle are to be expelled from the commonwealth.*

162. Statutes during the reign of Henry VII required laborers to work from daybreak to nightfall in spring and summer and from before 5 A.M. to between 7 and 8 P.M. in fall and winter.

163. Sidenote: *The work of laborers should be kept within bounds.*

164. Sidenote: *But nowadays playing at dice is the sport of princes.*

165. More surely knew how inaccurate Hythloday is here, since women in his time had duties at least as heavy as they have now.

166. That is, members of the religious orders.

167. Sidenote: *A very perceptive observation.*

168. This number would be made up of the governor, the two hundred syphogrants, the twenty tranibors, the thirteen priests, the scholars, and the ambassadors.

169. "Barzanes" derives from the Hebrew for "son of" and the Greek Doric form for "of Zeus." A Chaldean named "Mithrobarzanes" appears in Lucian's *Menippus*, which More translated. "Ademus" derives from the Greek for "without a people."

170. An average of twelve adults in each household would produce a population of seventy-two thousand in each city. Adding children and slaves would probably bring it to more than one hundred thousand (of whom only five hundred are exempt from work).

171. Hythloday's and the Utopians' rather facile justification of colonialism offers many difficulties. For example, if no one is using or occupying the land, why does anyone have to be driven from it by force? Is farming the only satisfactory use of land?

172. Sidenote: *Thus they avoid having a crowd of idle servants.*

173. That is, each of the four sides of a block has thirty houses, with a hall in the middle of each side.

174. Sidenote: *They always take freedom into account lest anyone act under compulsion.*

175. That is, without the help of servants.

176. Sidenote: *Praise and a sense of duty are the best way to encourage citizens to act properly.*

177. Sidenote: *The education of the young.*

178. Sidenote: *Priests above the prince, though nowadays even bishops are the lackies of princes.*

179. Sidenote: *Nowadays even monks rarely observe this custom.*

180. Sidenote: *Nowadays physicians condemn this practice.*

181. Cf. 2 Thess. 3:10.

182. Sidenote: *O holy commonwealth, worthy to be imitated even by Christians.*

183. Sidenote: *See how they never forget their sense of community.*

184. Sidenote: *What a clever fellow!*

185. Sidenote: *What a magnificent contempt for gold!*

186. Sidenote: *A very fine story.* "Anemolian" is from the Greek word for "windy."

187. Sidenote: *O what a craftsman!*

188. Sidenote: *He calls it dubious because the gems are fake, or at least because their glitter is scanty and dim.*

189. Cf. Lucian, *Demonax* 41; see also *CWM 13*, 8.

190. Sidenote: *How true and well put!*

191. Sidenote: *How much wiser are the Utopians than the general run of Christians!*

192. More uses "philosophy" in the older, broader sense of the investigation of all the arts and sciences, including mathematics and the natural sciences (which was often called "natural philosophy").

193. They have mastered the quadrivium, the second tier of university studies (music, arithmetic, geometry, and astronomy); of the first tier, the trivium (grammar, logic or dialectic, and rhetoric), dialectic is mentioned here. Grammar and rhetoric they would learn in their literary studies.

194. Sidenote: *There seems to be some underlying satire in this passage.*

195. Peter of Spain's thirteenth-century *Little Logicbook,* with its finespun categories and distinctions, was dissected and mocked by More in his *Letter to Dorp,* which he wrote in 1515, near the time he wrote the second book of *Utopia.* On complicated "rules about restric-

tions, amplifications, and suppositions" see More's text and Daniel Kinney's introduction to *Letter to Dorp* in *CWM 15*, liv–lvii, 29–39.

196. "First intention" refers to the intellect's direct perception of an object; a "second intention" is the intellect's perception of or reflection on a first intention. It has no objective existence outside the mind.

197. That is, the universal concept of man that applies to each man in particular. From the fourteenth century through More's time, scholastic philosophers from the camps of the Realists and the Nominalists quarreled elaborately about whether and how universals had any real existence.

198. Sidenote: *But nowadays these practitioners rule the roost among Christians.* More wrote a number of Latin epigrams ridiculing judicial astrology (*CWM 3/2,* 158, 166, 208, 214–16, 348–49).

199. Sidenote: *Natural science the most uncertain study of all.*

200. These three categories of goods (external goods and goods of the mind and of the body) derive primarily from the Aristotelian tradition. Generally the Aristotelians applied "good" to all three categories; the Stoics, only to the goods of the mind.

201. Sidenote: *The Utopians measure happiness by honorable pleasure.* That is, they are inclined to the Epicurean position that pleasure is the highest good. Beginning with Lorenzo Valla's *The True and False Good* (1444–49) and with the help of such thinkers as Ficino, Pico, and Erasmus, Epicurean philosophy had been rehabilitated and shown to consist not in mere hedonism but rather in the calm pleasures of the mind. But the Utopians differ sharply from the Epicureans, who did not believe in immortality and thought the gods were unconcerned about mankind.

202. Sidenote: *First principles of philosophy should be derived from religion.*

203. Sidenote: *The theology of the Utopians.*

204. Sidenote: *The immortality of the soul, about which not a few Christians nowadays have doubts.* The fifth Lateran Council (1513) affirmed as dogma the immortality of the soul. The philosopher most closely associated with the dispute concerning the immortality of the soul was Pietro Pomponazzi, whose treatise *On the Immortality of the Soul* (1516) argued that the doctrine could not be proved by reason but has to be derived from revealed religion.

205. Sidenote: *Just as not just any pleasure should be sought after, so too pain should not be pursued except for the sake of virtue.* This is in keeping

with the teachings of Epicurus; see Diogenes Laertius 10.130–32. The opposite faction is the Stoics.

206. Sidenote: *This is a teaching of the Stoics.*

207. Sidenote: *But nowadays some seek out pain, as if religion consisted in it, whereas pain is only to be borne if it occurs by natural necessity or to someone performing the duties of piety.* Seneca, whose Stoicism is often severe and uncompromising, agrees with the Utopians: "Our motto . . . is 'Live according to Nature'; but it is quite contrary to nature to torture the body, to hate unlabored elegance, to be dirty on purpose, to eat food that is not only plain, but disgusting and forbidding" (*Epistulae morales*, 5.4). Unlike some Stoics, Seneca is not entirely unsympathetic with Epicurus: "the teachings of Epicurus are upright and holy and, if you consider them closely, austere; for his famous doctrine of pleasure is reduced to small and narrow proportions, and the rule that we Stoics lay down for virtue, his same rule he lays down for pleasure—he bids that it obey Nature" (*De vita beata* 13.1). The Utopians combine elements of Stoicism and Epicureanism, and add to the blend belief in divine providence, the immortality of the soul, and rewards and punishments in the afterlife—doctrine not specifically Christian but not uniformly held until the advent of Christianity.

208. An Epicurean (not a Stoic) teaching; see Diogenes Laertius 10.138.

209. Sidenote: *A remarkable hypothesis, and a very apt one.*

210. More wrote a Latin epigram against the cruelty of hunters (*CWM* 3/2, p. 123).

211. Sidenote: *But nowadays this is the craft practiced by godlike courtiers.*

212. More is probably thinking of hunting dogs.

213. Sidenote: *This point should be noted with special care.* In *The Confutation of Tyndale's Answer* (1532–33), More argued on religious grounds that "besides the taming of the body, fasting and our pain taken therein pleaseth god done with devotion, and serveth us for obtaining many and great gifts of grace (*CWM 8/1*, p. 72).

214. Sidenote: *But nowadays blockheads and dolts are chosen to be educated; the most talented minds are corrupted by pleasures.*

215. The pupil and successor of Aristotle.

216. Constantine Lascaris (d. 1501) and Theodore of Gaza (d. 1475) wrote grammars of Greek. The dictionary of Hesychius (fl. ca. A.D. 400) was first published in 1514; Dioscorides (fl. ca. A.D. 50) wrote a handbook of medical and botanical terms.

217. Plutarch (ca. A.D. 50–120) was a favorite Greek writer among Renaissance humanists, both for his *Moralia* and for his *Parallel Lives* of eminent Greeks and Romans. Several pieces by the satirist Lucian (b. ca. A.D. 120) were translated by More and Erasmus and first published in 1506; they were reprinted ten times in the sixteenth century.

218. In the early sixteenth century the Venetian printer Aldus Manutius was famous for his compact, elegantly printed editions of classical authors in both Latin and Greek. In 1508 he printed the first enlarged edition of Erasmus' huge and elaborate collection of proverbs, *Adagia,* which brought Erasmus almost instant fame.

219. Thucydides and Herodotus are the leading historians of ancient Greece. Herodian (ca. A.D. 170–240) wrote a Greek history of the Roman emperors who reigned from A.D. 180 to 238.

220. A name in keeping with that of Hythloday himself: "tricae apinaeque" became proverbial meaning "stuff and nonsense" (Erasmus, *Adages* 143, *CWE 31,* 184).

221. Hippocrates (fifth century B.C.) and Galen (second century A.D.) were the leading Greek writers on medicine. *Microtechne* was a medieval summary of Galen.

222. Sidenote: *The remarkable fairness of this people.*

223. The non-hereditary character of Utopian slavery distinguishes it from both ancient slavery and feudal serfdom. In More's time it was generally agreed that Christians should not be enslaved, but the same was not true of African negroes and American Indians.

224. Such euthanasia, naturally, is contrary to Catholic teaching; at Morton's court Hythloday himself had said that God has forbidden us to kill ourselves (p. 27, above), but he also told More and Giles earlier that he did not intend to discuss whether or not Utopian moral principles are correct (pp. 91–92). More has a long psychological analysis of suicide in *A Dialogue of Comfort* (*CWM 12,* 129–56).

225. According to canon law in More's time, girls could not marry before the age of twelve and boys not before fourteen. Plato (*Republic* 5.9.460E, *Laws* 4.721A–B) and Aristotle (*Politics* 7.14.6.1335a) set the age of marriage for women at at least twenty and for men over thirty.

226. Sidenote: *This practice is somewhat immodest, but it is far from imprudent.* Plato requires similar premarital inspections in *Laws* 6.771E–772A, 11.925A.

227. In More's time the Church permitted separation in the case of adultery but did not allow remarriage. In his commentaries on 1 Cor. 7:10–11 and 39 Erasmus favored relaxing the prohibition of remarriage.

228. See Erasmus, *Adages* 1537 (*CWE 33*, 309–10).

229. The Latin for "fool" here is *morio*, wordplay on More's name; Erasmus had exploited the same pun in the prefatory letter of his *Encomium Moriae (The Praise of Folly)*, which is dedicated to More. Thomas More kept a fool, Henry Patenson, in his household; Patenson appears in Holbein's sketch of More's family and is mentioned by More in his *Confutation of Tyndale's Answer* (*CWM 8/2*, 900–901).

230. An error in the 1516 edition is corrected differently in the editions of 1517 and 1518, in both cases probably by More himself. One correction could mean that only crafty lawyers are excluded; the other must mean that all lawyers are excluded because all lawyers are crafty. The latter interpretation seems preferable.

231. The rulers and popes of More's time were notorious for breaking treaties or making them with the deliberate intention of breaking them. This was especially true of the popes Alexander VI and Julius II. Machiavelli said Alexander VI "never did anything, never thought of anything other than to deceive men. . . . And never was there a man who had greater success in asserting, and with greater oaths in affirming a thing, who observed it less" (*The Prince* 18).

232. A common false etymology derived "bellum" (war) from "belua" (beast)—or the other way around. For a full account of pacificism in More and his humanist contemporaries see R. P. Adams, *The Better Part of Valor: More, Erasmus, Colet, and Vives on Humanism, War, and Peace, 1496–1535* (Seattle: University of Washington Press, 1962).

233. One of the key texts giving the rules for fighting a "just" war was Cicero, *De officiis* 1.11.34–1.13–40.

234. Greek compounds meaning "cloud-born" and "citizens of a country without people."

235. From a Greek compound meaning "busy sellers"—that is sellers and resellers of their military services.

236. Sidenote: *A people not unlike the Swiss.*

237. Sidenote: *Above all the commander should be assailed so as to end the war sooner.*

238. A ducat was a gold coin minted primarily by Venice and worth about a quarter of a pound sterling at that time. The 700,000 ducats mentioned here would be worth many hundred times that much today.

239. The Utopians do not have an ordinary treasury; perhaps deposits owed the Utopians and placed in the treasuries of other countries are what is meant here.

240. Among the ancient Persians, Mithras was the supreme deity, identified with light.

241. Sidenote: *Monasteries.* Communism was practiced by religious orders in More's time, as it still is; on communism among the early Christians see Acts 2:44–45 and 4:32–37.

242. Of the seven sacraments, only baptism and matrimony can be administered by laymen.

243. In sacramental theology "character" is a technical term meaning the indelible quality bestowed on a soul by sacraments that cannot be repeated: baptism, confirmation, and holy orders.

244. Sidenote: *People must be drawn to religion by hearing it praised.*

245. In Christian England, More approved of punishing religious dissent or heresy, but that was because the true religion had been revealed there, as it had not in Utopia; as More said in *A Dialogue Concerning Heresies* (*CWM 6*, 345–46), "if it were now doubtful and ambiguous whether the church of Christ were in the right rule of doctrine or not, then were it very necessary to give them all good audience that could and would anything dispute on either party for it or against it, to the end that if we were now in a wrong way, we might leave it and walk in some better."

246. Sidenote: *A remarkable opinion about the souls of animals.*

247. In *A Dialogue Concerning Heresies* (*CWM 6*, 211, 213) More wrote concerning saints: "For if their holy souls live, there will no wise man ween them worse and of less love and charity to men that need their help, when they be now in heaven, than they had when they were here in earth. . . . When saints were in this world at liberty and might walk the world about, ween we that in heaven they stand tied to a post?"

248. Sidenote: *The active life.*

249. "Buthrescae" is a Greek word meaning "extraordinarily religious." In More's Europe the adjective "religious" was applied to members of

religious orders, who differed, however, from the Buthrescae in that they combined labor with prayer, study, and contemplation.

250. Hythloday must mean that the priests supervise the education of children, for in each city there are many thousands of children and only thirteen priests.

251. In *The Confutation of Tyndale's Answer* (*CWM 8/1*, 260–61) More accepts the traditional view that women may not be ordained as priests.

252. Sidenote: *But what a flock of them we have!*

253. Sidenote: *O these priests are far holier than ours!*

254. The first Greek compound means "dog days" (or perhaps "starting days); the second means "turning days."

255. There may be more than one service on every feastday, but even so the churches would have to be very large indeed: only thirteen of them serve about one hundred thousand inhabitants of each city.

256. Cf. Matt. 5:23–24.

257. Sidenote: *But among us the most defiled strive to get closest to the altar.*

258. Latin *superos,* which includes the one God, the other gods believed in by some of the Utopians, and their ancestors who are in heaven.

259. A startling idea, but perhaps Hythloday (or the Utopians) mean that for children this tends to be true.

260. In his *Four Voyages* Vespucci mentions that the American Indians made vestments of feathers.

261. Fr. Surtz notes that many of More's contemporaries, especially Erasmus, objected to the elaborateness of church music and urged that it be composed so as to emphasize the meaning of the words (*CWM 4,* 555–56).

262. Hythloday is so carried away that he speaks as if he is still in Utopia.

263. Goldsmiths often functioned as bankers.

264. Sidenote: *Note this, reader!*

265. Sidenote: *A striking phrase*

266. The remora has a suck-disk on top of its head, by which it attaches itself to larger fish or ships; impressed by its tenacity, the ancients thought it could impede the progress of a ship.

267. What "More" says here is in keeping with his earlier Aristotelian arguments against community of property. Aristotle continually associates nobility and the highest virtue with wealth; he defines magnificence as "suitable expenditure on a grand scale" (*Nicomachean Ethics*

4.2.1.1122a). But many readers get the impression that More lets the mask of the character "More" slip to reveal a hint of irony. For a discussion of the critical disputes about this passage see Thomas I. White, *"Festivitas, utilitas, et opes:* The Concluding Irony and Philosophical Purpose of Thomas More's *Utopia,"* *Albion* 10 (1978): 135–50.

268. This sentence is incomplete in the Latin and has been left so in the translation.

269. *Andria* 4.4.770–71.

Afterword

1. Clarence H. Miller, *Humanism and Style: Essays on Erasmus and More* (Bethlehem, Penn.: Lehigh University Press, 2011), pp. 105–7.

2. Jacob Burkhardt, *The Civilization of the Renaissance in Italy,* trans. S. G. C. Middlemore (1860; repr., Vienna: Phaidon Press, 1937).

3. See, for example, the following: Douglas Bush, *The English Renaissance and Humanism* (Toronto: University of Toronto Press, 1939); Paul Oskar Kristeller, *Renaissance Thought: The Classic, Scholastic, and Humanist Strains* (New York: Harper and Row, 1955); Charles Trinkaus, *The Scope of Renaissance Humanism* (Ann Arbor: University of Michigan Press, 1983); and Charles G. Nauert, *Humanism and the Culture of Renaissance Europe* (Cambridge: Cambridge University Press, 1995).

4. See Bush, *The English Renaissance,* pp. 13–38; Kristeller, *Renaissance Thought,* pp. 3–7; Trinkaus, *Scope of Renaissance Humanism,* pp. 3–31; and Nauert, *Humanism,* pp. 1–7. Nevertheless, the old idea of the medieval period as a "Dark Age" is not without its defenders. See Jack Goody, *Renaissances: The One or the Many?* (Cambridge: Cambridge University Press, 2010), p. 11.

5. See R. N. Swanson, *The Twelfth-Century Renaissance* (New York: Manchester University Press, 1999).

6. Burkhardt, *Civilization of the Renaissance,* p. 292.

7. Goody, *Renaissances,* pp. 5, 7–42. For an interesting study of the cultural energies released by print, see Alexandra Halasz, *The Marketplace of Print: Pamphlets and the Public Sphere in Early Modern England* (Cambridge: Cambridge University Press, 1997).

8. Bush, *The English Renaissance,* p. 82. For a helpful introduction to humanism in England, see Clare Carroll, "Humanism and English Literature in the Fifteenth and Sixteenth Centuries," in *The Cam-*

bridge Companion to Renaissance Humanism, ed. Jill Kraye (Cambridge: Cambridge University Press, 1996), pp. 246–68. For a circumstantial and critical history of humanism, see Anthony Grafton and Lisa Jardine, *From Humanism to the Humanities: Education and the Liberal Arts in Fifteenth- and Sixteenth-Century Europe* (Cambridge: Harvard University Press, 1986).

9. *The Basic Works of Aristotle,* ed. Richard McKeon (1947; repr., New York: Modern Library, 2001), p. 1329.

10. See John M. Perlette, "Irresolution as Solution: Rhetoric and the Unresolved Debate in Book I of More's *Utopia,*" *Texas Studies in Literature and Language* 29:1 (Spring 1987): 28–53. Perlette reads the debate in *Utopia* about the worth of advising a prince on public affairs as an extension of the ancient debate between Plato and the Sophists.

11. This is J. H. Hexter's coinage for the dialogue in Book I concerning the usefulness of advising a prince. See his *More's "Utopia": The Biography of an Idea* (New York: Harper and Row, 1952), p. 102.

12. Thomas More, "Letter to Martin Dorp," in *In Defense of Humanism: Letter to Martin Dorp; Letter to the University of Oxford; Letter to Edward Lee; Letter to a Monk, with a New Text and Translation of Historia Richardi Tertii,* ed. Daniel Kinney, vol. 15 of The Complete Works of St. Thomas More (New Haven: Yale University Press, 1986), pp. 26–39.

13. Lorenzo Valla, *On the Donation of Constantine,* trans. G. W. Bowersock (Cambridge: Harvard University Press, 2007), p. 73.

14. Harvey Cox, *The Feast of Fools: A Theological Essay on Festivity and Fantasy* (Cambridge: Harvard University Press, 1969), pp. 82–97. For helpful studies of the centrality of play to human life, see Johan Huizinga, *Homo Ludens: A Study of the Play Element in Culture* (Boston: Beacon Press, 1955), and Hugo Rahner, *Man at Play: Or, Did You Ever Practice Eutrapelia?* trans. Brian Battershaw and Edward Quinn (London: Burns and Oates, 1963).

15. Nauert, *Humanism,* pp. 5–6.

16. Peter Ackroyd, *The Life of Thomas More* (New York: Doubleday, 1998), p. 32.

17. Ibid., pp. 71–80. See also Richard Marius, *Thomas More: A Biography* (Cambridge: Harvard University Press, 1984), pp. 71–78.

18. Ackroyd, *Life of Thomas More,* pp. 82–95; Marius, *Thomas More,* pp. 83–87, 153.

19. See Hexter, *More's "Utopia,"* p. 99.

20. Alan F. Nagel, "Lies and the Limitable Inane: Contradiction in More's *Utopia,*" *Renaissance Quarterly* 26:2 (Summer 1973), pp. 175–77).

21. See the essay "Editions of *Utopia*" by Edward Surtz, S.J., in *Utopia,* ed. Edward Surtz, S.J., and J. H. Hexter, vol. 4 of The Complete Works of St. Thomas More (New Haven: Yale University Press, 1965), pp. clxxxiii–cxciii; and R. W. Gibson and J. Max Patrick, *Thomas More: A Preliminary Bibliography of His Works and of Moreana to the Year 1750 with a Bibliography of Utopiana* (New Haven: Yale University Press, 1961), pp. 3–57.

22. It is striking that in his early twenties, More delivered a series of lectures on St. Augustine's *City of God.* See Ackroyd, *Life of Thomas More,* pp. 104–6.

23. See Hexter, *More's "Utopia,"* pp. 85–96; Marius, *Thomas More,* pp. 67–69; and Ackroyd, *Life of Thomas More,* p. 99. Hexter clarifies that there are also groups within Utopia who live a professed life that more closely resembles monasticism.

24. *The Rule of St. Benedict,* trans. Anthony C. Meisel and M. L. del Mastro (New York: Image Books, 1975), p. 106.

25. More's Latin, along with a prose translation, appears in Clarence H. Miller et al., eds., *Latin Poems,* vol. 3, part 2, of The Complete Works of St. Thomas More (New Haven: Yale University Press, 1984), pp. 238–41.

26. The quotation comes from the Arden edition of Shakespeare's *The Tempest,* ed. Frank Kermode (London: Methuen, 1954), 2.1.153–54.

27. In his *More's "Utopia"* (Toronto: University of Toronto Press, 2000), Dominic Baker-Smith emphasizes More's concern with what modern theology has identified by the term "social sin," the distortions of human values woven into the social fabric. See pp. 115–16.

28. The phrase comes from Bernard Lonergan, *Insight: A Study of Human Understanding* (1957; repr., Toronto: University of Toronto Press, 1992).

29. Lewis Mumford, *The Story of Utopias* (New York: Peter Smith, 1941), p. 78.

30. Besides his introduction to this edition, see also Clarence H. Miller, *Humanism and Style,* pp. 71–79.

31. Elizabeth McCutcheon, "Denying the Contrary: More's Use of Litotes in the *Utopia*," in *Essential Articles for the Study of Thomas More*, ed. R. S. Sylvester and G. P. Marc'hadour (Hamden, Conn.: Archon Books, 1977), p. 263.

32. Stephen Greenblatt, *Renaissance Self-Fashioning: From More to Shakespeare* (Chicago: University of Chicago Press, 1980), pp. 22–26.

33. See Miller's *Humanism and Style*, pp. 71–79.

34. Ibid., 76.

35. Ibid., 72.

36. William Roper, *Sir Thomas More*, in *Two Early Tudor Lives*, ed. Richard S. Sylvester and Davis P. Harding (New Haven: Yale University Press, 1962), p. 198. With regard to More's devotion to the theatrical metaphor, see Greenblatt, *Renaissance Self-Fashioning*, pp. 26–37. See also Thomas More, *The History of Richard III*, ed. George Logan (Bloomington: Indiana University Press, 2005), pp. 94–95, 126–28.

37. See Dominic Baker-Smith, "'*Civitas philosophica*': Ideas and Community in Thomas More," in *A Companion to Thomas More*, ed. A. D. Cousins and Damian Grace (Madison, N.J.: Fairleigh Dickinson University Press, 2009), pp. 165–77.

38. The use of the term "relationism" as a way of understanding the sociology of knowledge emerged in the work of Karl Mannheim; see his *Ideology and Utopia: An Introduction to the Sociology of Knowledge* (New York: Harcourt, Brace and Company, 1936), pp. 71–78 and passim. Among more recent scholars, the one who has done the most, as far as I know, to develop the implications of the term is Walter J. Ong; see his *Fighting for Life: Contest, Sexuality, and Consciousness* (1981; repr., Amherst: University of Massachusetts Press, 1989), pp. 29–34; and "Hermeneutic Forever: Voice, Text, Digitization, and the 'I,'" *Oral Tradition* 10 (1995): 3–26. See also my "Ong, Evolution, and the Method of Dialogue," *Explorations in Media Ecology* 9:1–4 (2010): 103–18.

39. For further considerations, see Charles Trinkaus, "The Question of Truth in Renaissance Rhetoric and Anthropology," in *Scope of Renaissance Humanism*, pp. 437–449.

40. Bernard Lonergan, *A Second Collection*, ed. William F. J. Ryan, S.J., and Bernard J. Tyrrell, S.J. (Toronto: University of Toronto Press,

1974), pp. 1–9. See also Anthony Grafton, *What Was History? The Art of History in Early Modern Europe* (Cambridge: Cambridge University Press, 2007).

41. For helpful insights into such dialogue, see David M. Bevington, "The Dialogue in 'Utopia': Two Sides to the Question," *Studies in Philology* 58:3 (July 1961): 496–509.

42. Martin Waldseemüller, *Cosmographiae Introductio,* trans. Joseph Fischer and Franz von Wieser (University Microfilms, 1966), pp. 91–97.

43. Ibid., p. 98.

44. Roper, *Sir Thomas More,* p. 198. See also Ackroyd, *Life of Thomas More,* pp. 96–101.

45. *Rule of St. Benedict,* ch. 33.

46. *Collected Works of Erasmus: Adages Ii1 to Iv100,* trans. Margaret Mann Phillips (Toronto: University of Toronto Press, 1982), p. 29.

47. Kathy Eden, *Friends Hold All Things in Common: Tradition, Intellectual Property, and the "Adages" of Erasmus* (New Haven: Yale University Press, 2001).

48. All references to Aquinas are to *Summa Theologica,* 3 vols., trans. Fathers of the English Dominican Province (New York: Benziger Brothers, 1947).

49. Paul Ricoeur, *Lectures on Ideology and Utopia,* ed. George H. Taylor (New York: Columbia University Press, 1988), p. 310.

50. Ibid., p. 311.

51. Ibid., p. 312.

52. See Walter J. Ong, S.J., *Interfaces of the Word: Studies in the Evolution of Consciousness and Culture* (Ithaca: Cornell University Press, 1977), pp. 166–81; and Halasz, *Marketplace of Print.*

53. Hanan Yoran, *Between Utopia and Dystopia: Erasmus, Thomas More, and the Humanist Republic of Letters* (New York: Rowman and Littlefield, 2010), p. 63.

54. Ibid., pp. 177–86.

55. See Walter J. Ong, *Ramus, Method, and the Decay of Dialogue: From the Art of Discourse to the Art of Reason* (1958; repr., Chicago: University of Chicago Press, 2004), pp. 307–18.

56. For a fine introduction to these and related themes in the work of Jacques Derrida, see his "Structure, Sign, and Play in the Discourse

of the Human Sciences," in *Writing and Difference,* trans. Alan Bass (Chicago: University of Chicago Press, 1978), pp. 278–93.

57. Jacques Derrida, *Negotiations: Interventions and Interviews, 1971– 2001,* trans. Elizabeth Rottenberg (Stanford: Stanford University Press, 2002), pp. 13–14.

58. I would like to thank Amanda Joyce, Mike Smolinsky, and Mary Szybist for their helpful comments, as well as my students Charlotte Markle and Justine Minette for their hours of helpful conversation about More's *Utopia.* The errors and folly are mine.

UPDATED BY JERRY HARP

BIOGRAPHIES

Ackroyd, Peter. *The Life of Thomas More* (New York: Doubleday, 1998). The most reliable full biography.

Chambers, R. W. *Thomas More* (London: Jonathan Cape, 1935; repr., Ann Arbor: University of Michigan Press, 1958). A classic biography, well informed and beautifully written, but it neglects the polemical works.

Guy, John. *Thomas More* (New York: Oxford University Press, 2000). Emphasizes especially the political struggles. Guy acknowledges that some issues that have exercised More biographers cannot be resolved based on the available evidence; thus, as he points out, each reader tends to make More over into his or her desired image.

Marius, Richard. *Thomas More: A Biography* (Cambridge: Harvard University Press, 1984). The biography that makes the most extensive use of the full range of More's writings. Marius performed a helpful service by writing against the grain of the hagiographic tendencies of past More biographies, though his conclusions occasionally overreach the evidence; he rides his hobbyhorse a bit vigorously at times.

Roper, William. *Sir Thomas More,* in *Two Early Tudor Lives,* ed. Richard S. Sylvester and Davis P. Harding (New Haven: Yale University Press, 1962). A handy edition of the first biography of More, written by his son-in-law—personal and poignant.

BIBLIOGRAPHIES

Geritz, Albert. *Thomas More: An Annotated Bibliography of Criticism, 1935–1997* (Westport, Conn.: Greenwood Press, 1998). Excellent, very full. Pages 215–309 are devoted to *Utopia* alone.

Gibson, R. W., and J. Max Patrick. *Thomas More: A Preliminary Bibliography of His Works and of Moreana to the Year 1750 with a Bibliography of Utopiana* (New Haven: Yale University Press, 1961). Early editions and translations of *Utopia* up to 1750.

Lakowski, Romauld Ian. "A Bibliography of Thomas More's *Utopia,*" http://extra.shu.ac.uk/emls/01-2/lakoutop.html. This excellent Internet bibliography, devoted exclusively to *Utopia,* also exists in a printed form: *Early Modern Literary Studies* 1.2 (August 1995).

Wentworth, Michael D. *The Essential Sir Thomas More: An Annotated Bibliography of Major Modern Studies* (New York: G. K. Hall, 1995). Entries 380–640 are devoted to *Utopia* alone.

The indices of the journal *Moreana* will provide a plethora of articles on *Utopia.*

EDITIONS
Utopia: Latin Text and English Translation, ed. George M. Logan, Robert M. Adams, and Clarence H. Miller (Cam-

bridge: Cambridge University Press, 1995). A reliable and usable Latin text, with a compact introduction and notes.

Utopia, ed. Edward Surtz, S.J., and J. H. Hexter, vol. 4 of The Complete Works of St. Thomas More (New Haven: Yale University Press, 1965). Full-fledged edition with elaborate introduction, textual variants, and a very full commentary.

L'Utopie de Thomas More, ed. André Prévost (Paris: Mame, 1978). The French equivalent of Surtz's edition, with a facsimile of the edition of November 1518, an elaborate introduction, a French translation, and a very full commentary.

Utopia, trans. Ralph Robinson, Everyman's Library (New York: Alfred A. Knopf, 1992). The first English translation. This edition includes a helpful introduction by Jenny Mezciems.

STUDIES OF *UTOPIA*

Baker-Smith, Dominic. *More's Utopia.* (Toronto: University of Toronto Press, 2000). A multidimensional introduction. Baker-Smith discusses the historical background and literary precedents in detail. He shows the continuing relevance of the work, especially with regard to what he terms social sin, the injustices woven into the social fabric.

Bevington, David M. "The Dialogue in 'Utopia': Two Sides to the Question," *Studies in Philology* 58:3 (July 1961): 496–509. Emphasizes the open-endedness of the dialogue that *Utopia* invites the reader to join.

Cave, Terence (Ed.). *Thomas More's "Utopia" in Early Modern Europe: Paratexts and Contexts* (Manchester: Manchester University Press, 2008). Provides studies of the material—e.g., prefaces, poems, essays, letters—that accompanied early editions of *Utopia* in a variety of languages.

Cousins, A. D., and Damian Grace (Eds.). *A Companion to Thomas More* (Madison, N.J.: Fairleigh Dickinson University Press, 2009). Brings together studies ranging from the early epigrams to the Tower works.

Greenblatt, Stephen. *Renaissance Self-Fashioning: From More to Shakespeare* (Chicago: University of Chicago Press, 1980). Explores the unstable and distorted relationship between the two books of *Utopia,* which Greenblatt also connects to More's role-playing.

Hexter, J. H. *More's "Utopia": The Biography of an Idea* (New York: Harper and Row, 1952). A detailed study of the evolution of *Utopia.*

Logan, George. *The Meaning of More's "Utopia"* (Princeton: Princeton University Press, 1983). Provides a close reading of *Utopia* as a product of Northern humanism, with constant reference to the classical and medieval antecedents, as well as contemporary influences.

Logan, George M. (Ed.). *The Cambridge Companion to Thomas More* (Cambridge: Cambridge University Press, 2011). A collection of essays on More's life and writings, by some leading More scholars.

McCutcheon, Elizabeth. "Denying the Contrary: More's Use of Litotes in the *Utopia,*" in *Essential Articles for the Study of Thomas More,* ed. R. S. Sylvester and G. P. Marc'hadour (Hamden, Conn.: Archon Books, 1977), 263–74. Demonstrates the significance of More's frequent use of litotes in *Utopia.* As a figure of discourse, litotes allows a more complex understanding than simple affirmation or negation can accomplish.

McCutcheon, Elizabeth. *My Dear Peter: The "Ars Poetica" and Hermeneutics for More's "Utopia"* (Angers: Moreanum,

1983). An excellent study of litotes and the oblique style of *Utopia.*

Miller, Clarence H. "Style and Meaning in More's *Utopia:* Hythloday's Sentences and Diction," in *Humanism and Style: Essays on Erasmus and More* (Bethlehem, Penn.: Lehigh University Press, 2011). Demonstrates the significance of the shifts of style in Hythloday's Latin.

Nagel, Alan F. "Lies and the Limitable Inane: Contradiction in More's *Utopia,*" *Renaissance Quarterly* 26:2 (Summer 1973), pp. 173–180. A consideration of the contradictions, tensions, and impossibilities woven into More's text.

Nelson, William (Ed.). *Twentieth Century Interpretations of Utopia: A Collection of Critical Essays* (Englewood Cliffs, N.J.: Prentice-Hall, 1968). Provides a broad range of commentaries and perspectives.

Perlette, John M. "Irresolution as Solution: Rhetoric and the Unresolved Debate in Book 1 of More's *Utopia,*" *Texas Studies in Literature and Language* 29:1 (Spring 1987): 28–53. A reading of the Dialogue of Counsel as an extension of the ancient debate between philosophy and sophistry.

Sylvester, Richard S. "'Si Hythlodaeo Credimus': Vision and Revision in Thomas More's *Utopia,*" *Soundings* 51 (1968): 271–89. Reprinted in *Essential Articles for the Study of Thomas More,* ed. R. S. Sylvester and G. P. Marc'hadour (Hamden, Conn.: Archon Books, 1977), pp. 290–301. The best brief introduction to the ironies of *Utopia.*

Sylvester, R. S., and G. P. Marc'hadour (Ed.). *Essential Articles for the Study of Thomas More.* (Hamden, Conn: Archon Books, 1977). A collection that lives up to its title.

Yoran, Hanan. *Between Utopia and Dystopia: Erasmus, Thomas More, and the Humanist Republic of Letters* (New York:

Rowman and Littlefield, 2010). A study of the early humanists' desire to create a virtual community transcending national boundaries and institutional affiliations, and the impossibility of doing so. Yoran provides a reading of *Utopia* in light of this impossibility.

INDEX